# SURVIVING LIFE
# BEYOND THE PALE

# SURVIVING LIFE
# BEYOND THE PALE

## I Was Set Up!
## A journey from innocence through abuse to strength.

M.A. Sandry

Grateful Steps
Asheville, North Carolina

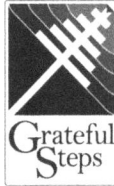

Grateful Steps Foundation
Crest Mountain
30 Ben Lippen School Road #107
Asheville, North Carolina 28806

Library of Congress Control Number: 2020938170

Sandry, M.A.
*Surviving Life Beyond the Pale:*
*I was set up! A journey from innocence*
*through abuse to strength.*

Cover illustration by Ollyy,
purchased from Shutterstock

ISBN 978-1-945714-39-9 Paperback

Printed in the United States of America
at Lightning Source

FIRST EDITION

gratefulsteps.org

iv

To the angels who helped
me survive and to others
on their own journeys

# Author's Note

This story is a condensed version of my life, one that I felt compelled to write. First, as a cathartic experience to provide some psychological relief through expression. Second, to provide insight into the tragedies of childhood abuse. Even when a child is born into a normal, well-adjusted family, things can go wrong. It serves as a warning to parents as well. Actions and inactions can and do affect children's entire lives. It is a true story.

\* \* \*

My mother rocked me as a small child without demonstrative affection. Touch was not her thing. I later thought if I could understand her, then I'd be closer to understanding myself. She was often absent, bringing home small presents of apology. I hated to see her angry or sad. Sweet-smelling Tea roses grew along the fence leading down a steep hill from our house to the road. When I picked the flowers, I garnered my courage, fearful that I could tumble down the incline to my death. Gathering a bouquet of roses in my child fist and wincing when a thorn stuck, I crawled back up to the house. By presenting my mother with this bouquet, I hoped to ease her emotions and beg for forgiveness if I had caused her pain.

My mother was not a fan of sex. She told me that my nipples were "to help you breathe." My next-door neighbor, a dear childless woman, taught me about menstrual cycles and bought my first belt and sanitary napkins. Apparently, my father was not receiving what he needed in the sex department. His secretary was a younger woman whose interests in my father were way beyond bookkeeping. In time, he noticed and eventually ran off with her. My mother was not a happy person. "Oh, dear," was what I often heard. I loved my mother. But we would never be friends. She was even jealous of me. Why not? Her second husband, my stepfather, often said that he wished he could have married me. Even though I needed a father, my stepfather was repulsive to me, and after he sexually molested me, he was not even a man in my eyes, but a monster.

Before my father left, life was wonderful for me as a child. But then, suddenly, he was gone. I remember that when he watched TV, he always sat in a large, red, leather chair studded with brass tacks along and down the arms. The arm rests were stained dark from use. After he left us, I often climbed up into the seat and sank into the hollow impression made by his hours of watching his favorite programs. I snuggled into it and inhaled the fragrance of leather and stale cigarette smoke, then stretched my hands out to both sides, my fingers barely touching the arms. I imagined my daddy's arms there. I wrapped my own arms around myself in a ghost of a hug from him.

I grew to late childhood without any positive relationship models. No one ever told me that they were proud of me or encouraged me in school. I was not taught how to succeed. I was in my early 40s before I felt like a "grownup." As a child, I had been groomed only to be promiscuous. I became promiscuous searching for a father figure. I self-medicated with drugs to deal with my loss and confusion. I did not seek counseling; I did not know that it existed for me. Only when I repeated my story over and over again did I finally hear it for myself . . . and understood. It took years.

Dear Reader, You must summon your courage to face the pain needed to find the solution for a normal life. You must tell your story. This is mine.

# CONTENTS

Author's newlywed parents
with her paternal grandparents.

## CHAPTER 1

# Innocence Exploited

I WAS AN EMBARRASSMENT FROM THE START. MY MOTHER'S water broke while the congregation was standing to pray. My father quickly ushered her down the aisle, leaving a wet trail of amniotic fluid in their wake. That was difficult to explain. My father with face flushed, a half smile curling his lips, supported my mortified mother past the murmuring parishioners.

My first breath was taken in a small hospital snuggled in the heart of the Blue Ridge mountains. My mother told me that it had cost my parents $75.00 to pay for my delivery. Of course, that was in the 1950s. Life was easier to manage on one income then.

Mishaps did not end there. My father's sister and her husband, along with my paternal grandmother, piled into their Model T Ford and rushed to the hospital as soon as they had word of my delivery. Screeching up and around a mountain curve, my uncle lost control. The Model T almost ran off the side of the mountain but was fortunately hindered by a large oak tree. The only damage sustained was a bent fender and my Aunt Ella Mae's broken wrist. Without auto damage enough to disable the car, they continued to the hospital. There my aunt's wrist was splinted, and they were all able to ooh and aah at me through the glass window of the nursery. My father, Harry, who had been delegated to the smoky waiting room until after the birth, was also among the grinning throng of relatives.

I was named Elaine after my mother instead of Harry, after my father. Thank goodness, I had been born a girl! After a week in the hospital, my mother and I could go home. It had been an uncomplicated delivery. There I was introduced to my 7-year-old brother, Lee.

Author's brother.

He had not been allowed to visit us in the hospital; remember, it was the 50s. He was not

2

ever very thrilled at having a baby sister. After all, he had been the only child for seven years. It was later, when I was old enough to walk and talk, that I can remember how he tormented me, teasing me by pretending our attic was haunted and using my baby dolls as baseballs.

I was a Carnation milk baby. The doctor told my mother that her breast milk was "too thin and blue" to nourish me. In that era, doctors were not educated about nursing mothers. So much for the DHA protein that is found in breast milk and has been shown to help infant brain and retina development. It had not yet been added to formula. I was missed for ideal brain development. I was also exposed to narcotics. My mother was told by my doctor to give me paregoric for colic, teething or just plain fussiness. It was an exempt narcotic that contained forty-five percent alcohol and two milligrams per five milliliters of opium. To give it to a child today would be considered child abuse. Could a schedule III narcotic given in childhood be related to drug use later in life? If so, I was set up then. My parents did not need a prescription; the pharmacy just sold it over the counter. I can still remember the taste of it, and the euphoria it induced, as I became older.

* * *

My very first memory was of a very hot summer day. I woke up alone in the backseat of our 1956 Chevy, the seat sticky and wet from my sweat and drool. The window was open, and I could hear laughing and people talking but could not see anyone. The car was parked in the driveway behind our house. My family were in the front yard with the neighbors. The door handle was too stout for my small hands to grip, and as I struggled to open the door, I screamed for my mother. It seemed like an eternity, but finally my mother appeared, running around the corner of the house, face flushed. When she opened the door to my interment, she cooed apologies into my damp hair. I could smell the cigarettes and the sweet faintness of bourbon in her jet-black hair. The grownups were having a cook out with the neighbors, enjoying their afternoon toddies, and had forgotten about leaving a sleeping 3-year-old in the car.

I cannot remember ever riding in a car seat. The cars back then had no seatbelts . . . and certainly no laws regarding child safety. When I sat in the front with my mother while she ran errands, whenever she had to stop, she put out her arm in front of me to keep me from flinging into the dashboard of the car. It became such habit, she continued to do this for years later after I had grown, and seatbelts were the norm. Other times, when all the family members were in the car, I preferred to climb up onto the back-window ledge. From that vantage point, I could see the tops of trees rushing by overhead. I made faces at the people in the car behind us.

Our family outings were wonderful. Just a quick trip to Lord's Drugstore was always a sure thing in scoring a double-dip, butter pecan, ice cream cone. It is the same place my mother got paregoric that she used to sedate me when she couldn't handle me. I still remember the paregoric causing floating, nothing bothering me, not scared of getting in trouble. We went to Lake James every summer. My parents had a motor boat and diving gear. We stayed at Green's boat dock in a rock house. My best friend in the world at that time was Sylvia Green. We were the same age, 6 or 7. We chased fairies in the woods and tadpoles in the shallows of the lake. As a child I was happy and truly believed in woodland fairies and loved reading about them from the age of 5. But at home there seemed to always be underlying tension . . . not overt. My father had anger issues. My mother was always nervous, always agreeing with my father, never wanting to "rock the boat." Even as a child I felt she was too compliant. Looking back now, I can see that my mother was living in a toxic, abusive relationship with my father. My maternal grandmother lived with us and essentially raised me because my mother took a job outside the house.

Author's maternal grandmother.

One afternoon I almost drowned. My parents were on the shore at Lake James. They were at a fire pit laughing and having their afternoon toddies. I had ventured too far out into the lake. My feet were touching the bottom, then suddenly, they weren't. My head went under, and I began to thrash and gurgle screams,

6

sometimes surfacing and going under again. I could see my folks on the bank, but they didn't appear to be alarmed. They were not watching me; they were talking to another couple who had just arrived. My toes curled and sought the sandy bottom while my head went under once more. Miraculously, my big toe of my right foot snagged onto a submerged branch, and my other foot found the bottom. Gasping, I managed to find my footing and tiptoe to shallow water. No one ever knew. I was afraid to tell because I thought I would get into trouble. Shaken, I found a sandy towel and sat down beside the fire to dry off and to calm myself. I made up my mind to learn how to swim that summer.

My dad and my older brother would skin dive and ski on the lake. I was told that I was too young, I would have to wait until I was 10 or 11. I never went diving or skiing. My father left us the spring before my 10th birthday.

My father was a dental technician. He was of short stature with a short temper. He fashioned partials and dentures for the dentists in the area while smoking unfiltered Lucky Strikes one after another and indulging in "toddies for the body" regularly. He made a decent living, as far as I could tell. We had a new car every year. A speed boat and a motorcycle sat in the garage. We lived in a lovely two-story house sitting on a hill surrounded by three acres of land.

My parents were often absent, my mother working at the county courthouse registering deeds. My father was busy at his lab . . . and busy with his secretary. My grandmother, Jessie, took me to church every Sunday. We were Southern Baptists. Everyone else belonged to a cult, in her opinion. Two weeks out of the summer, I attended Vacation Bible School until I was too old.

Author with her dog, Baby.

Life was good then. I had the freedom to roam the woods with my collie, "Baby." She was my constant companion. A family moved into the house beside ours, separated by an old chicken wire fence. The family of six were apparently very poor. The two younger children were always dirty with ill-fitting, stained clothing. My grandmother forbade me to talk to them, but we met, the chicken wire separating us, and managed to engage in childhood fantasies. The summer foliage concealed us.

When the family of six finally moved on, a childless couple moved into the house. Raymond and Francis became good friends with my parents. They spent almost every weekend twilight cooking out in their front yard, drinking and laughing. One such evening, while unsupervised, I once discovered and captured a cat, or so I thought, and put her inside a grocery box. When my father lifted the box, he quickly put it down and exclaimed "that's a wharf rat!" They all then proceeded to pour gasoline onto the box and set it on fire. Astonished, I stared at the blaze until I couldn't tolerate the shrill cry of the poor burning creature and ran. I was probably about 6.

I spent a great deal of my time at the neighbors' house. Without any children of their own or illicit affairs to distract them, they lavished their attention on me. I drank Pepsi over a glass of cracked ice and learned to love sardines between two saltine crackers while watching the Flintstones cartoons on their color TV. I usually sat on the floor in front of the TV. Sometimes I cuddled in Raymond's lap while he smiled. He often shared a bowl of popcorn with me. My father never held me. I craved the attention. Being the medically inclined, curious 6-year-old that I was, I scanned Raymond's shadow-bearded countenance for individualized bumps and black-filled craters. I maneuvered my dimpled fingers on either side, and by applying pressure, achieved a satisfying gush or plug of debris. He didn't mind me doing this.

This story triggers another memory: I was also curious about the blood stream, apparently. My earliest tries at phlebotomy were attempted upon the large night crawlers in my yard. Unbeknown to my grandmother, while she taught me how to thread a needle and weave the finer stiches, she was also suppling my first medical supply kit.

My maternal grandmother and I shared a bedroom. She was older than my paternal grandmother. She had been in her 40s when my mother, the youngest of 12 children, was born. My mother confessed to me that she was ashamed of her mother for being so much older than the other mothers of her classmates.

I adored my Grandmother Jessie! She taught me how to grow a garden, can tomatoes and make "leather britches"—a way to preserve green beans by stringing them up to dry. We kept chickens for their eggs and for tasty Sunday dinners of fried chicken.

I was traumatized when I witnessed her snatch up an unlucky hen by the neck. With a quick twist, she broke its neck and popped off its head. The poor thing scrambled around the yard then, sans head, pumping chicken blood from the severed neck until, ensanguined, it collapsed dead. A large galvanized tub of steaming hot water waited on the porch. She dunked the chicken in and out of the water until the feathers were loose enough to pluck. I can still smell the aroma of wet chicken feathers when I close my eyes and remember. I was not one to let my squeamishness deny me the culinary pleasure of my grandmother's fried chicken! I do miss her.

She had her own way of disciplining me. A God-fearing Christian, she believed that to "spare the rod was to spoil the child." I was often too engrossed when I played in the woods with my dog, Baby. Out of sight and barely within hearing range, I heard her calling me. Too often I tarried and received her punishment for it. She sent me to fetch a hickory switch, and if it wasn't one to her liking, she fetched a bigger one. Most of the summer, I wore marks on my legs where she had switched them.

Never squeamish herself, Granny was the first one to grab a hoe to kill the rattlesnake unfortunate enough to cross her path. I believe I learned how to be strong from her.

My paternal grandmother, Ruby, had a nice one-bedroom trailer on the lower lot of our property. Ruby was a flapper in her youth during the "Roaring Twenties." Always a wild child, she conceived my father out of wedlock. That secret, kept within the family, was always a sore spot with my father. She married Jesse Ferguson, who then adopted my father. I remember her relentless enthusiasm about life, especially on Christmas morning. She ran to our house and wakened me, squealing, "Santa Claus has been here! Quick! Get up! He brought you the doll you wanted!" I could tell by my mother's expression, that she wasn't very happy that Grandmother Ruby had spoiled the surprise.

Ruby was a smoker, and I suspect had passed down that habit and the propensity for "adult beverages" to my father. Early one morning, I woke to the sound of an explosion. Apparently, my grandmother had fallen asleep with a cigarette and had also left the gas stove on. I ran to the back door to see my father running down to the blazing trailer. The blast had ripped off the back of the trailer, and my father emerged, carrying my grandmother from danger. Unharmed, but for singed hair, and coughing from smoke, both my father and his mother were okay. The trailer was a complete loss. Remnants of heat warped kitchenware, glass cracked, and blackened, and cold embers were found scattered about my woods for several years afterward. Grandmother Ruby moved to Greensboro after that instead of moving in with us. My mother would only tolerate one grandmother in the house.

Author's parents, 1950s.

My father spent more and more time away from home. There were days that he was absent from the dinner table. My brother didn't adjust very well to this because he had all my father's attention when my father was home, and he blamed my mother and me for the lack of fatherly attention. During one screaming match between my mother and my brother, I was in the line of fire. He picked up a cast-iron frying pan, snatched me up by my hair and threatened to "bash my brains out." That's all I remember. My mother must have backed down, and he must have let me go, my skull intact.

My father's absence was due to his secretary, a saucy young woman with her mind made up to marry him. He found with her the passion that had apparently been missing in his marriage. I sometimes overheard my grandmother talking over the phone in hushed tones, that my father and Sallie were "shacking up." All I knew was that he was no longer living at home. This added to the complex trauma, resulting in my psychological numbing.

When he finally realized that besides leaving my mother, he was neglecting his children, he began to take us for the weekends. He had rented a small summer cottage on top of Beaver Dam Mountain. There he taught me to shoot a .22 rifle, a present for my tenth birthday. I was a good shot. After a while, he took me squirrel hunting. While we were in the woods, he pointed up into a tree and said, "There's a perfect gray squirrel for you to shoot."

The squirrel was looking at me. I aimed the rifle, but I couldn't shoot. I lowered my rifle and looked up at my father.

He shook his head and, without a word, took the rifle away from me . . . permanently. I regretted disappointing him. It took away any time that he spent with me.

My father and Sallie lived on the mountain for a year. He encouraged me to invite my friends over and even paid for a party. I'm not sure why. I invited all my friends and their friends. A local, live band played while my father allowed us to indulge in beer. I was 11 years old.

One afternoon he drove up in a brand new, baby blue, 1964 Mustang 2+2, and told me it was mine. I was thrilled, although I would have to wait until I was old enough to obtain my driver's license. His lover didn't appreciate the attention I was receiving. I woke up the next morning to the news that she had driven the Mustang down the mountain, not on the gravel road, but through the trees. She had sustained a few scratches but had totaled my first car. I was not there for what I am sure was a "knockdown, drag out" fight between my father and her after that escapade. I was told she was "drunk as a skunk" at the time. Apparently, they reconciled and left the next week for California. My father never mentioned the offense I had suffered and never bought me another car.

Before leaving with his lover for California, my father had not only left us, he claimed bankruptcy. The family home was taken by the bank and put up for auction. My sweet home and the three acres sold for $10,000. Even then, in 1963, that was a deal. The four of us—my mother, maternal grandmother, brother and I—moved into a rented house inside the city limits.

The new house was a sweet little thing—older, two stories with three bedrooms, and an arbor covered with ivy and roses at the front door. And there were neighborhood kids to play with! I had been virtually isolated before. My only playmates, my dog and the "poor-white-trash" kids who had lived briefly across the fence in the house next door.

Here there were children living in almost every house. My best friend, DeeDee, lived on the opposite side of the street, a couple of houses up the hill. We had strung a cord on a pulley with which we sent notes to each other. The neighborhood kids fashioned skate boards from old skates and scrap wood from the remodeling of a neighbor's house. The ice cream truck would wake us from our make-believe revelry to scramble home, begging quarters from our parents' purses. Troll dolls came into fashion, and an entire summer was spent in a fantasy world with my blond, bubble-cut haired, bikini-clad Barbie and the Trolls.

My brother attended the local university and brought friends home with him. The slicked-back hair of the 50s gave way to the cleaner crew cut. The house was full most every weekend with crew-cut heads and rock n' roll. I realized that I was growing up when one of these crew cuts made a pass at me. My developing body was attracting unwanted attention. It wasn't all bad. My friend DeeDee and I had fun flirting with the college boys. We accepted frequent offers of joy rides in their convertibles, relishing the freedom of the wind in our hair, the smiles and compliments we received.

Author's mother.

My mother was lonely. I occasionally caught her crying, and she always passed it off as "something in my eye." She soon started dating. Her constant companion was Bill Wilson. I found out later that he was my paternal grandfather. I suppose that she was trying to embarrass my father. Or perhaps she saw the image of my father in his face. When I looked at him, I saw an older, gruffer solid reflection of my own lost parent. I am sure that she always loved my father.

To further complicate the issue, Bill's daughter, Mary, who was really my aunt, watched me while the two of them went out. She was 18 and as wild as my Grandmother Ruby. She dressed my 16-year-old-appearing body in one of her provocative outfits and put make up on my 11-year-old face while we listened to the latest Beach Boys hit "Little Duce Coup" on the AM radio. I was having the time of my life hanging out with her. I felt so grown up and sophisticated.

I experienced my first kiss, sitting in the back seat of her 1960, red Impala. She had met two of her "guy friends" at Buck's Drive-In. After inviting them to join us, we drove up to Beaucatcher mountain and parked overlooking the city lights below. The guy sitting in the backseat with me put his arms around me and without saying a word, pressed his mouth to mine and slid his tongue inside my mouth. Startled, I bit it. Sandra and her guy friend had a big laugh all the way back down the mountain. The guy I had bitten, sullen, holding a handkerchief to his bleeding tongue wasn't laughing. I wasn't laughing either. I was embarrassed almost to tears. I didn't stay with Mary much after that. My mother broke up with Bill soon afterward. She had been home sick in bed for a week, pale, shaking and with vaginal bleeding. I never learned why.

The next man in my mother's life was Al. He had known my mother since they were children frequenting the swimming pool at Beaver Lake in the 1930s. They had lost track of each other after grammar school. I'm not sure how they met up again. He eventually married her, and he was Pop Pop forever afterward. He was a jovial person, almost always smiling.

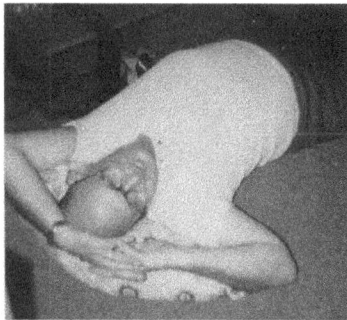

Author's stepfather.

19

Claiming to be a reverend by profession, he certainly belied that notion by exhibiting hedonistic behaviors. He was always eager to show off his newest car. My favorite was his red Ford Fury. Talk about a muscle car! My mother and I frequently sneaked out after Al had passed out from drinking. She would often relent and let me drive that car. We went to Buck's Drive-in on Tunnel Road to check on my brother and his escapades. Sometimes we ran into Billy and Ruth Graham there having hamburgers and fries with their family.

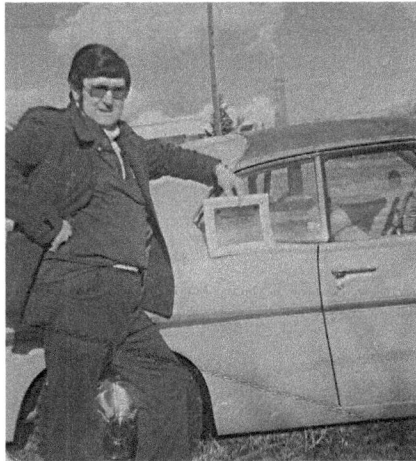

Author's stepfather
displaying his seminary diploma.

Al was bald, but wore a toupee all the time. His sideburns gave him an Elvis look. I remember catching him using my mother's mascara on them to cover the gray. He seemed very vain. He bragged about knowing movie stars and was a regular at Francis Langford's casino in Fort Pierce, Florida. Jackie Gleason was a close drinking buddy of his.

At first, he treated my mother like a queen, buying her clothes and taking her on vacations. When my mother obtained a divorce from my errant father, she married Al. Things changed then. He insisted that my grandmother move out of "his" house. She went to live with her son, my Uncle Richard, and his wife.

Author at age 12.

The drawback from my grandmother leaving was now that my mother had to stay home with me while he went on his vacations to Florida without her. She was still working at the county courthouse, while he was mostly "between jobs."

During the school year, this arrangement worked because she continued at her job while I was in school. Summer vacation came, and Al was relegated to caretaker of a 12-year-old girl, me.

He always welcomed my girlfriends over and encouraged sleep-overs. He popped popcorn and gave us sodas, mixed with alcohol, to drink. The 35mm movie camera appeared, and we were more than eager to show off. It was fun. We were wearing our nighties and were unconscious of our budding breasts because we were so young. It was fun jumping up and down together on the bed. It didn't seem creepy at first, but when he suggested that we hug and tickle each other, it became embarrassing. Before my mother was expected to come home from work, he would quickly clean up, washing the glasses and putting the camera away.

One day while we were home alone together, he began talking to me about my boyfriends. He questioned me if we ever kissed and if we had done anything besides kissing. He then proceeded to give me a lesson on how a girl and a boy "date." I was appalled, and when he started touching me, I hit him. He grabbed my panties and ripped them off. Screaming at him to leave me alone, I picked up the closest weapon at hand, a poker from the fire grate. He quickly backed off and left me alone. I was still alone when my mother arrived home from work. Sobbing, I told her what had happened and even showed her the ripped and ruined panties. She looked away from me and told me calmly that she didn't believe me. I was devastated. I knew then that my mother would always defend him.

After that, he would come into my bedroom after I was asleep to fondle me. I would wake up to his fingers between my thighs. He would leave me when I woke up. I never knew when I went to bed at night if I would wake up from being molested. He continued these occasional night visits until I was sent to California to live with my father.

I never had a real father in my life. I know now that I was desperately looking for a father figure, given the unfortunate series of men in my life. My misperceptions equating lust for love and over-reacting to innocent events, such as my startle reflex with noises at night, were the direct result of the acute trauma of my father's abandonment and my stepfather's inappropriate attention.

\* \* \*

That, I believe, set the stage for the rest of my life—being victimized and not knowing what to do about it. I was not rescued.

CHAPTER 2
## *Springtide*

WITH MY FATHER IN CALIFORNIA, MY MOTHER PRE-
occupied with my pedophile stepfather and my
brother away at college, I was left to my own
devices. Being older—all of 12 years of age—my
girlfriends and I noticed boys. I had freedom to
roam the neighborhood without supervision. After
all, it was the 1960s. I rode my bike to the school's
basketball courts and met two or three girlfriends.
There we watched the boys play. We giggled and
flirted behind curtains of our silky blond and soft
curly auburn hair. Some college students from
the nearby university had apartments on the hill,
affording more freedom and privacy than living in
the dorms. Taller, muscular and definitely more
mature than our male counterparts, they sprinted
across the court, battling for possession of the
ball. I can recall the fragrance of the pheromones
that filtered through the warmth of the summer
breeze. So exciting and sweet, stirring our bodies

with unfamiliar urges. The more grownup and manly the boys were, the more interested I was.

It was the 60s; "free love" was the cultural norm at that time, rebelling against our parents' stogy and insincere attitude towards morals. Virginity was a profane title. It seemed that most of my friends had shed theirs, or at least claimed to have, and I was anxious to join them in becoming an adult. One of the college boys flirted back with me. He was fourteen years older, and I was starved for his attentions. We often went up the hill from the basketball court to his apartment and listened to his collections of 45 rpms. One afternoon we took it to another level. I had anticipated this, and the champagne he provided helped sooth my nervousness. He had also put a chicken on the hibachi. With candles glowing softly, it seemed like a real grow-up date! Listening to "Good Lovin'" by The Young Rascals on the stereo, we kissed and then eventually found ourselves fumbling with our clothes. Pleasure quickly turned to pain. I scrambled up, hurt, embarrassed and deflowered. I felt the specter of my stepfather, laughing, sinister from the corner of the room.

The summer ending soon with crimson leaves and cooler breezes, my Romeo moved back on campus. I never saw him again. But youth has a way of renewing itself. The next two years were filled with friends who remain so to this day. School was located downtown close to the courthouse where my mother worked. My friends, "flatty Patty" and Sherry, and I would walk over to see her for money. Always generous with money in lieu of affection, she gave me a few dollars, and we walked up to Cosmos, a local café and hangout, ordered a huge plate of fries to share and Cokes, while we talked and flirted with the boys. This was truly my late childhood, filled with Halloween haunted houses in a friend's basement and drinking wine while playing Monopoly with a boy who was from France, my Barbie dolls in the corner but not forgotten.

Always restless, my parents moved me with them to Fort Pierce, Florida, that winter to escape the cold. My brother was now in college in Tennessee. My stepfather was closer to his buddies, Frances Langford and ol' Jackie G. We didn't see a lot of my stepfather, much to my relief. When he was at home, he was still sneaking into my room at night to fondle me while I was sleeping. Other than that, life was good in Florida. My friends Gloria, Hazel and I skipped down the sandy road alongside the beach, parroting the Monkees, singing their theme song, arms clasped around each other, legs overlapping with each gleeful step. We went fishing for sharks off the public pier, using huge hooks baited with moray eels. Gloria had biker friends. We tore off down the beach on the guys' Harleys, spraying sand and laughing at our freedom. My parents didn't seem to notice my absences for long hours at a time, being occupied with . . . what I couldn't care less! I became friends with the next-door neighbor boy, and my friendships with the girls took a back seat. We were the same age, 14, he was tall, six feet, seven inches, with sandy blond hair—shot through with platinum streaks from the sun—falling over sky-blue eyes. He was a drummer, and the rhythm issuing from his downstairs room thrilled me when I touched the wall with my fingertip. His attention brought the male figure that had been missing from my life.

Finding ourselves unsupervised, we spent all day on the beach or in the pine woods behind our apartments. I had been initiated into sex earlier than he was, but it didn't take him long to catch up. I remember singing "Eleanor Rigby" while we ran laughing to our hiding spot underneath the trees dripping with sap. Intimacy was so sweet with him. I had found my first real love. School out, the spring was filled with just our courtship. Summer arrived and found both the berries ripe in the field between the beach and woods and myself ripe with child. I told my lover and he told his mom. Taking me aside, she handed me five dollars and told me never to see him again. I tried to call him, but he wouldn't answer me. I was heartbroken. I decided that I wasn't pregnant and denied the whole thing to myself. I didn't tell my mother and stepfather. I mourned the loss, but told myself that there were plenty of men in the world, and someday I would be special and cared for by one.

One day soon after, my mom decided that she had had enough of my stepfather. "Pack up your things, we're leaving," she told me. Loading up her car with our scant belongings, she looked over her shoulder with dread and spun out of the driveway. I had been aware that she had been agonizing over the decision to leave, but this was so sudden. We left the car at the Greyhound Bus Station. Without any discussion for the next twelve hours, we reached North Carolina. She rented a small basement apartment in town and went back to work at the courthouse.

It was summer, and with no school, I soon had rounded up some of my old friends. I was greeted with, "Hey, kid, where have you been?" Other than that, it was as if I had never left. We lived only a few blocks from The Brass Tap, the local tavern." Even though I wasn't old enough to drink legally, the owners were friends of mine. They looked the other way when I sipped from the glasses of all my friends who were older. The alcohol helped with my anxiety. I must have still had monthly bleeding, but due to stress and denial, I didn't even notice. It must have been very scant. I don't remember needing a Kotex pad. My hormonal drives were noticeable. I was more than anxious to get together with an old boyfriend. Before, we were just good friends—he was a couple of years older than me, most of my friends were. Now, we became more than friends. Intimacy was fantastic! We spent most of our time together.

CHAPTER 3
# California

SUDDENLY ONE DAY, I FOUND MY SUITCASES PACKED AND my mother in a flustered state. My stepfather had found us and had convinced my mother to reconcile. I was in the way, and I guess he was tired that his efforts to rape me were ruined by my waking up and threating to scream. They took me to my cousin's home. My stepfather walked me to the door. He got back in the car and sat behind the wheel. My mother wouldn't look at me as they drove away and left me there without even saying how long I would be there or even goodbye. My dad had received a phone call from my stepfather telling him a lie, that I had run away and that no one knew where I was. After calling relatives, my father located me at my cousin's home and promptly sent me airfare. I arrived at LA International and was greeted by my angry father and my aggravated, evil stepmother, who had always despised me.

My father and stepmother were living right on the beach in Newport. It was a sky-blue cottage with vaulted ceilings. A white, wind-weathered fence separated us from the pedestrians on their way to the surf that we could hear from our back deck. The sand on the deck reminded me of the snow that I thought I'd never see again. I preferred to go to the beach at Newport pier, only a few blocks down. There the flower children were in full bloom. Music flowed and mingled with the sound of the surf. The Doors and Donavan at times competed with and at times blended with each other. The aroma of fresh bread and marijuana filled every deep breath. Life was good away from home, but a hard-labor prison at my father's house. I was responsible for all the house work. If the ash trays were not sparkling or the pots had a spot of grease, my stepmother made me do everything over again. School started, and I found more friends. Everyone was tanned, and mostly blond hair glinted in the sun. I made the faux pas of asking on the first day where the restroom was and was informed that it was called the head, not restroom. I also made a spectacle of myself when spying a classmate across the campus and calling out, "Hey, ya'll." Everyone within earshot turned and laughed. Nonplussed, I responded, "I'm from Asheville, ya'll!"

My father had an old army friend, Jerry. His wife, Mary, and my father and stepmother often got together at our house to play cards, smoke and drink. On several occasions, Jerry excused himself to find me. Cajoling me to take a sip of an "adult beverage," he slipped his arms around me and forced his tongue into my mouth. He tasted like cigarettes and whisky. I would gag and turn away, but he just laughed and told me, "You know, you are the sweetest girl." Even when he repulsed me, he could make me feel special and loved by paying attention to me. He asked me how my day was, how school was, what my interests were.

Sometimes, I was already in my bed asleep when they played cards late into the night. I would startle awake with Jerry's hand down the front of my pajamas and his fingers prodding into me. I knew it was wrong. I knew that telling wouldn't help me. I had told my mother about my stepfather's abuse. She said, "I don't believe you." I had told my stepmother, when she was living with my father near my home in Asheville. She had said, "That's terrible. Your father will take care of it. Nothing was ever done. I knew that no one cared, except for maybe Jerry. He didn't stop until things changed, and they did when his wife began dying of cancer. They moved to be closer to her oncology treatments. I never saw him again.

My waist expanding, I began to wear a girdle, a staple in those days. My father noticed and confronted me. "What have you been eating, girl? Or are you knocked up?"

I did not have an answer for him about my weight gain, so he took me to a doctor. I was stunned and relieved when I heard the doctor tell us, "Your daughter is around seven months pregnant."

I think I just shut down, no feeling, no pain, no hurt, no happiness, just a numbness. They took me out of school. My father was embarrassed and so angry with me. My stepmother referred to me as "your whore daughter" while smirking behind my father's back.

"We have to move," my father told her. "She can't be around anyone we know here." This caused my stepmother to hate me even more; she loved her beach house. When my father wasn't home, she often hit me and kicked me until I hid under the table. She would then spit curses at me. "You've ruined my life!" she fumed. "We had a great thing here. Now your father must start somewhere else because of you, you slut!" She added, "You're ruined! No man will ever want you now."

We left the house on the beach and moved inland to another school district. The house was roomy, enough room to be able to avoid my father and my stepmother. But it was gloomy with shadows in every corner. Sided with dark green and surrounded by eucalyptus trees, the house admitted sunlight scantly through the windows. There were plenty of places to hide.

I enrolled in my new school, not showing enough to be obvious. People just thought that I was plump. I didn't mind, and I reinforced the image by devouring a chocolate malt at every break and at lunch. I was craving them. At home I stood at the freezer door, chomping on ice cubes. My stepmother forced me to continue wearing the girdle. "The longer you can get away with it, the better off you'll be."

I was in algebra class when I first acknowledged that I felt the baby move. I was still in denial; I thought the feelings were a bad case of gas. In a month or so, the gas pains became more frequent . . . and more frequent, every ten minutes or so.

In a few days, I was hiding under the table, gasping with each wrenching twist of pain and with my stepmother laughing at me. I hoped my father would come home and he finally did. He noticed me gasping underneath the table. "What is going on here?" he asked my stepmother.

"I believe the little bitch is in labor. Serves her right," she replied. "At least we will have a baby out of this mess."

I didn't know what she meant until in the midst of labor at the hospital, someone shoved a pen and clipboard into my hands. In between contractions my stepmother told me, "You can have something for the pain when you sign this paper." Not knowing what it was and feeling the beginning of another wrenching pain, I scribbled my name. The pain was horrible. Especially that I didn't know what was happening to me. I screamed during every contraction and wept and gasped between them.

Finally, the doctor came into the room. "Sit up and bend over, arch your back," he told me. I felt a pinch, then a cooling sensation crawling down my spine, then no sensation at all below my waist. He had given me an epidural. Thankful for the respite from the torture, I fell asleep.

I woke up lying on a cold table being prodded by a masked figure. "The pelvis is small, too small to deliver vaginally. We may have to perform a C section," the masked figure said.

Another figure, this one female, replied, "Let's take an x-ray to determine if the baby has enough room to be born vaginally first." That's all I heard, drifting down into blackness once more.

I woke covered with stiff hospital sheets and a light cotton blanket. The gripping pain was gone, replaced by a stinging soreness between my legs. I looked around, still groggy. I was alone. I felt my stomach, once round and hard like a watermelon under my shirt, now still bloated, but soggy, like watermelon gone to rot. I then felt a gush of warm liquid rush out from between my legs, wetting the pads beneath me. I attempted to get up from my reclining position to go to the bathroom. But when I sat up, the room started to spin a bit. Light-headed, I swung my legs over the side of the bed just as a nurse came in the room. "Oh no, don't get up, child." When she saw the blood running down my legs onto the floor, she pushed the emergency call light and quickly, after pushing me back onto the bed, began to massage my stomach. "She's hemorrhaging!" she told another nurse who had poked her head into the room. It was only after a few minutes—thanks to a needle injection in my thigh and with the nurse's hand still on my now-clenched uterus—that the flow of blood subsided. Another needle, this one in the arm, and all was oblivion again.

I was in the hospital for three days. Not in the maternity ward, but in a private room on another floor. The only person to visit me was an old friend of my father. He was from Tennessee, and I am not certain that he was real or whether I dreamed his visit. On the third day, a nurse came into my room with a wrapped bundle in her arms. After lying the pink-blanketed form on the bed in front of me, she unwrapped it to reveal the most beautiful baby I had ever seen. Astonished, I started to weep. "She looks like me!" I choked out. "Can I touch her?"

The nurse smiled sadly and, looking behind at the closed door, nodded.

Gathering the sweet bundle into my arms, I kissed the downy head and plump cheeks.

"She weighs ten pounds and is twenty-one inches long," the nurse told me. I had all of fifteen minutes to meet and say goodbye to my daughter. I had been told that the papers that I had signed while I was in labor were legal documents that relinquished my parental rights. My stepmother and my father were the legal parents. The birth certificate had their names listed as the mother and father. Not mine. They had stolen my child from me.

It was hospital policy for a discharged patient to be escorted to the front door in a wheelchair. I was sitting in the wheelchair, my stepmother and father walking behind me, when a sweet nurse brought the baby out to us. She put the baby into my arms. My stepmother's mouth opened, and she screamed, "That is my baby! Don't give it to her!" She bent down and whispered in my ear, "And if you ever say any different, I will cut your throat with a rusty knife." That was not the last time I would hear that oft-repeated threat.

The nurse turned to her and calmly replied, "It is hospital policy that the birth mother carries the baby out of the hospital, ma'am." She smiled at me.

Fuming, my stepmother stomped to the car and jerked open the door. Snatching my baby out of my arms, she snarled, "That is the last time you'll hold her!" Infant car seats were not required in those days. Holding my newborn daughter, my stepmother cuddled and cooed to her while I cowered silently in the back seat. It was December in Southern California, sunny and mild. But I was chilled through to my soul.

\* \* \*

Christmas was only days away. My breasts were swollen, sore and hot. Milk wept from my nipples. My body grieved as though my baby had died. I was numb. Only when I heard her cry, I would wake as if from a bad dream and remember that she was alive. My only connection to her was washing the residue of cereal thinned with formula from her bottles and laundering her soiled diapers. True to my stepmother's word, I was never allowed to hold her. I would sneak into my stepmother's and father's bedroom, when they were distracted elsewhere, and lean over the crib to watch my daughter sleep.

Christmas morning dawned. A set of cheap suitcases were under the tree with my name on them. "Thank you, but what are these for?" I asked my stepmother.

"I thought that you could use them," she replied. That night I couldn't sleep for the hushed arguments I heard coming from their bedroom. The next day when I got home from school the suitcases were packed.

My father was still at work. My stepmother met me at the door. She handed me fifty dollars and my suitcases and told me, "You can go stay at one of your friends for a while . . . or forever if you want to. But you must go."

Shocked and not moving, I stared at her.

"I mean it, your father and I need some time together without you around."

So, I, a 15-year-old girl, went stumbling down the road.

CHAPTER 4
# Beyond the Pale

THE OFFICIAL RECORD WAS THAT I HAD BEEN ABSENT from school two weeks with "mono." Now it was Christmas vacation, and I had another week to figure out what I was going to do. I hoped that my friend Laurie and her mom would take me in. Their house was within walking distance. Laurie was in my homeroom at school. Her hair was blond, almost white from hours spent on the beach underneath the California sun. With brilliant white teeth in an ever-open smile, she was the most joyful person I had ever known, a beauty, standing all of four feet. I towered above her at five. Her mother was a free-spirited, single mom, the epitome of a bohemian\hippie. Herbs hung from the kitchen rafters. Incense and candles wafted exotic fragrances throughout the house. Beautiful poster art—such as a reproduction of Gismonda by Alphonse Mucha, and Bob Massa's colorful rendition of Janis Joplin at the Avalon

Ballroom—hung on the purple painted walls. Laurie's mom greeted me with a smile and asked me if I were hungry. She created a sandwich for me made from home-baked, whole grain bread, spread with almond butter and stuffed with alfalfa sprouts and avocado.

The sunny, blue skies of Southern California and the mild climate allowed Laurie, her mom and me to tie-dye cloth on the front lawn. "Don't fret over your stained fingers, girls," Laurie's mom laughingly told us. "Hands and fingers are beautiful no matter what color they happen to be!"

We hung our creations—in hues of cardinal crimson, bruised purple, baby-chick yellow and Christmas-tree green into patterns resembling swirling clouds from space—on the line to dry in the warm, fitful Santa Ana winds. I remembered my stitches taught to me by my maternal grandmother so long ago and made halter tops from the dried cloth.

* * *

The rest of the winter months passed as if in a dream. Laurie's mom was my mom, always there, loving us. My body healed, and my soul was comforted. There was never an issue with school regarding why I was not living at home with my legal guardians. No one ever asked. I guess they didn't know that I had been kicked out, and I never said anything.

* * *

The winter rains ceased and the green hills above the sandy beaches slowly burned to rust underneath the warm sun. School was out, not that it meant much to me. I had been skipping classes for months. Laurie's mom didn't seem to care, or maybe she just didn't notice from within her pot-induced euphoria. Laurie and I had been spending more and more time hanging out at the neighbor's. The pot was plentiful, and the two brothers who lived there with their two moms were generous.

Yes, I had been introduced and immersed into the California drug scene. We lay around the small trailer that sat in the neighbor's yard. The windows were covered with tapestries from India, and beaded curtains hung from the doorway. Candles were the only illumination. We listened to Grace Slick of the Jefferson Airplane belt out "White Rabbit" while we passed a joint around. Every so often, some long hair sporting leather and beads would drop by with hash, reds (a prescription barbiturate) or psilocybin mushrooms. I didn't touch the reds, but had a blast on several psychedelic mushroom "trips."

Of course, I was young, healthy and curious. I was also attempting to self-medicate. The drugs helped me forget most of what I had endured in my young life.

*  *  *

The next two years were a blur. I went from place to place, crashing wherever I could. With no money, I depended on the generosity of my fellow hippies and God. Most people shared what they had. Every now and then, several days went by with nothing else to eat but a loaf of white bread. It lasted me almost a week unless I shared it with another hungry person. Occasionally, I begged enough coins to buy Pop Tarts. They were always a treat. My friend stole sandwiches from the 7-Eleven when we didn't have enough money to buy them. Drugs were always available for free. The only thing that helped me face life was pot. Everything else was too intense . . . also frightening.

I even tried heroin. A group of people were using a cheap motel room for the evening debauchery. I had been drinking brandy and was definitely drunk. I looked down at my arm and saw that a rubber hose was tied around it. Someone was thumping the crook of my arm. "To bring up your vein," they told me. Someone else was holding a spoon over a flame from a lighter. Brown liquid bubbled from the heat and crusted around the edge of the spoon.

Using a syringe, the person who had tied my arm and thumped my vein drew up the liquid from the spoon and stuck the needle into my vein. When he pulled back on the plunger, I saw bright red blood mingled with the brown. He had a look of concentration on his face. "Good, I did it," he said. Then the contents of the syringe disappeared into my arm. Within seconds, everything seemed to slow down. My tongue felt thick in my throat and I got a taste I haven't forgotten yet.

I stumbled into the bathroom and gagged dryly as my stomach lurched. Once was enough. I felt sick the rest of the night, lying in a fetal position at the foot of a bed.

I no longer hung out with that crowd.

I hung out at the beach mostly. Listening to the sound of the waves lapping, sometimes crashing onto shore, subdued my anxiety. I could then mellow out enough to sleep on the warm sand without nightmares.

I was staying at a commune at one point. It was a cute cottage. Surrounded by a flaking, white, picket fence and profusely growing, scarlet blooming, California wild poppies, the cottage hid an interior of amazement. The women—dressed in long, flowing skirts of rainbow hues, wearing handmade halter tops of lace or no top at all—were usually busy chasing tousled hair, barefoot, naked toddlers, or baking confections laced with marijuana. The men were reticent, lying around the sparsely furnished living room most of the day on piles of colorful pillows. My job was to weed the small vegetable garden behind the cottage. I filled my mouth with juicy red tomatoes and sighed with pleasure as the tangy, sweet juice filled me. Whenever I could stay away from the salacious men that were always hanging out, I felt almost at home.

The coterie of hippies grew larger, bringing people I had never seen before. One evening, a long-haired man with bells around his neck burst through the front door. His pupils were so dilated that his eyes looked black. "I've got the good stuff!" he blurted out on sweet, yet rancid-smelling breath. "There are enough hits for everybody! Let's party!" He held out an envelope filled with small glassine packages. Inside each one was a small square with the image of a rabbit. "LSD," he said. I had been smoking pot that day and had eaten a brownie or two, so I was willing to participate.

Someone told me to stick out my tongue. She gently placed one of the rabbit squares on the tip. We settled down to listen to music and passed a joint around. The smoke from the burning pot drifted up and mingled with the candlelight, creating prisms of color on the faces next to me. I looked around at the group of people sitting—some lying supine—and noticed three men across from me. Two were smiling at each other, not saying a word, but I could hear their conversation. "Hey, just look at these sweet, young girls we have here! What do you want to do with them?" The one with the scraggly beard smirked.

"We can think of something cool, dude."

The third man holding a joint replied. "Hey man, that chick there can hear us!" he said, as he looked my way and caught my eye.

Suddenly, I was alone in the room, standing above a forced air vent that was blowing my skirt around me in billowing colors. A man was sitting across the room from me, back against the wall, knees askew and grinning at me. "What do you think of my world?" he asked me.

Startled and disconcerted at the sudden change of venue, as well as the ominous presence of this figure, I gathered my courage and replied, "Your world is like a paper bag, enclosing falsehood and easily escaped. Get behind me, Satan." And with those words, he vanished, and I found myself lying on my sleeping cot. I prayed, thanking God for his mercy and for looking out for me. The rest of the night passed with tranquil music in my mind.

The next morning, I grabbed my small tote of belongings, slung it over my shoulder and left the cottage unaccosted. Finding a pay phone at the street corner, I dug a dime out of my bag and dialed my father's number. He answered on the third ring. Forgetting the anguish I had experienced at home, I broke down and cried, "Dad, I need you."

"Okay, I'll come and pick you up. Where are you?" he asked. I told him and sat down on the curb to wait.

It seemed like forever, but he finally drove up next to me. "Get in." he told me and drove me to a motel. "I've paid for two nights here. Here's twenty dollars." He opened my car door, and after I stepped out, he drove away.

Alone in my motel room, I ran to the bed and threw myself onto it. Too stunned to cry, I sobbed dry gasps. My birthday was in a week. I would be 17.

CHAPTER 5
# The Duck Test

I WOKE UP TO THE NOON SUN SHINING IN MY FACE. Walking to the window, I could see Disneyland in the distance. I remembered the times my hippie friends and I went there, sneaked in and smoked pot between rides. I didn't know where any of those friends were and didn't know how to get hold of them. I was alone.

The bathroom had clean, white towels and soap. Thrilled, I took a long, hot shower. Hungry, I pulled my halter top over my head and my bell bottom jeans up to be fastened at my hips. I went to find something decent to eat. I had the twenty dollars that my father had given me, but I had to be thrifty if I was going to make it last.

Closing the door to my motel room behind me, I heard laughing and smelled perfume through the half-opened door down the hall. Three women emerged. They were dressed in short, tight skirts, wearing high, spiked heels and a lot of makeup.

Glancing at me, one with long, platinum blond hair smiled. "Hi, sweetie," she greeted me. "Where did you come from?" Then eyeing me more closely, she said, "You look like you could use a meal. We are on our way to get a bite of lunch. Care to join us?"

Preferring company, I told her yes.

We sat down in a booth in a nearby restaurant that catered to the tourists. Dumbo the elephant was on the front of my menu while Mickey Mouse goofed from across the table on my hostess' menu. Searching the list of burgers and fries selections, looking for the cheapest, I saw that Doreen, the platinum blonde, noticed my hesitation.

"Don't worry honey, I've got this." I was moved to tears, and when I could catch my breath, I told them my story.

"You're so pretty, sweetie, and with nicer clothes, some makeup and something done with your hair, you'd make a lot of money," the redhead named Tina told me. "We three girls live together. This is the week that the navy is in town, so we're here to work. We have a nice house down in San Diego. We have enough work there, but this is a working vacation for us."

"Oh, yeah. We'd be glad to help you out. We'll teach you how. It's easy money!" Mary the short-haired blonde told me.

Grateful for my new friends, I thanked them for lunch, told them that I didn't think that I could do that kind of work and said goodbye.

* * *

I had one more day paid for at the motel. I knew I had to make the best of the respite. Grabbing a discarded newspaper from the lobby, along with a cup of black, hours-old coffee, I went back to my room to look through the want ads for a job. A listing for help wanted at a nursing home caught my eye. "Needed immediately for elder care. Sign-on bonus given. No experience necessary." The address was within walking distance. Quickly, I washed my face and ran a comb through my hair. Everyone looks lovely at seventeen years of age. No makeup needed.

Walking down the sidewalk felt more like drifting, effortless, infused with hope that maybe now I would be able to afford to take care of myself. It was a beautiful day. The sun was shining through the leaves of the eucalyptus trees overhead. The warm ocean breezes kissing the leaves, caused dancing patterns from the shadows that the sun cast.

The quarter mile walk was over quickly, and I found myself in front of an ivy-covered threshold. A feeling came over me . . . something in my life was about to change. Opening the door, I immediately noted that my olfactory nerve was assaulted by a faint malodorous smell. It seemed to be a mixture of stale urine, the cabbage that was served for lunch and Clorox. Turning to survey my surroundings, I saw that the room was furnished with a sagging couch gladdened with brightly flowered pillows. Two comfortable side chairs and a coffee table adorned with a large vase of flowers completed the décor. A sliding glass portal to my right revealed a smiling woman rising from her chair in front of a typewriter.

"Hello. Can I help you?" she asked, as she stepped from her office into the entrance area where I was standing.

"Yes, "I replied. "I'm interested in the position listed in the paper."

Still smiling, the woman went back into her office and returned with a folder. Handing it to me, she said, "Just have a seat and fill out the application and income tax forms for me."

Taking a pen from the jar holding a variety of pens and pencils, I sat down and began the process that would change me from a child into a woman. When I had finished filling out the paperwork and handed it back to her, she asked me to wait. Nervous yet excited, I sat back down. I didn't know what to expect, and when she returned with even a brighter smile, I felt my apprehension fall away.

"Can you start today?" she asked me. "We had someone call out and could really use you." I nodded my head, and she continued, "We provide your uniform, so if you will follow me, I'll get you set up."

She returned with blue scrubs.

The rest of the day was filled with learning the job requirements. I was paired up with a matching, blue scrub-clad woman, Gloria. She wasn't much older than myself. She showed me where the clean cloth diapers were kept and where to wash out and put the soiled ones. Handing me a stethoscope, she asked me, "Do you know how to take vital signs? If not, I'll teach you."

I learned so much that first day and was shown so much compassion.

At the end of my shift, I changed my clothes, hugged Gloria, said goodnight to the residents I had cared for that day and left with a heart full of hope.

* * *

When I arrived back at the motel, the belongings that I had left in the room were on the floor outside my room, the door locked. My time was up. My father had paid for only two days. Weary,

I slumped down in front of the locked door. Just then, my neighbor Doreen was opening her door. When she saw me, she asked, "What are you doing, sweetie?"

I told her that I didn't have any money for another night's motel rent, but that I had a job now. "I was so excited to get this job, I completely forgot that my room was for only two days. I don't know what to do now . . . I'm just so tired."

"Oh, sweetie, you can stay here with us for a few days. We'll be here until the Navy gets their notice to ship out." Smiling, she opened the door wider. "Come on, there is a fold-out cot that you can rest on."

Gratefully, I picked up my meager belongings and followed her into the room. Another fragrance wafted by me, a mix of musty sweet perfume and stale cigarette smoke. The bed was strewn with rhinestone-studded dresses and fur throws. I almost tripped over stiletto-heeled shoes.

"Oh, do be careful! Those are Christian Louboutin! They are worth more than you are!" Doreen screeched.

Admonished, I carefully stepped around the glossy red shoes. "Sorry. They're beautiful," I croaked out. Clearing my throat, I asked, "Are you sure that's it's okay with the other girls that I crash here?"

"Oh, sure honey. We have another room that the johns pay for if they want to party," Doreen answered while pouting her lips and applying another layer of crimson lipstick. "In fact, I'm on my way out, so you have the place to yourself for most of the night. Just make yourself comfortable, but don't touch anything," she said, turning around to face me. No longer smiling, she continued, "You can sleep here for a night or two, but if you cause any problems, well, there's the door."

"Thanks, Doreen, I'll keep to myself. You won't even know I'm here. I really appreciate your kindness." Sitting down on the plastic and metal chair by the orange Formica table, I folded my hands in my lap and tried to sink into myself.

Plastering a smile on her made-up, slathered-although-expertly-applied face, she grabbed a fur wrap. "Okay then, squirt, be good." After turning the door handle to open the door, she stepped out into the balmy Southern California evening to meet her date.

Sighing, I stood up and surveyed my surroundings. The two king-size beds dominated the room. Both were unmade and were scattered with embroidered, lace-hemmed peignoirs and stockings. Crystal-topped perfume bottles, lipsticks, eyeshadows and other sundries crowded the bathroom vanity. Housekeeping had not been there in a while it seemed, as soiled towels littered the bathroom floor. Turning back to the bedroom, I decided to watch TV and try to relax. Unfolding the cot, I found a pillow and blanket inside. I pushed the cot as far into the corner of the room as I could, praying that I would be out of the way when my benefactors came back. Weary, I stretched out on the cot and plumped up the pillow under my head.

The next thing I became aware of was bright rivulets of sunlight shining on my eyelids. It was early morning. I had slept through the night without dreams or awareness. My roommates were asleep, draped across the king-size beds. Looking at the clock beside the nearest bed, I saw that I had an hour to get up and ready for work. I have a job! A legitimate job. After a quick shower, I dried off with a damp towel I found slung over the door knob to the bathroom. I jerked on my clothes . . . still crumpled even though I had hung them up the night before. I jogged the quarter mile and stopped short to catch my breath before opening the door to the nursing home. The familiar tang hit my nose. The cabbage replaced with bacon. So much better.

Gloria greeted me as I was changing into my uniform in the employee's lounge dressing room. "Hi!" She greeted me, smiling. "Back for more, I see."

"Yep, I think I'm going to like working here," I greeted her back. "The old people are so sweet."

"Ok, you think so? Good. I'll introduce you to Alma today. She is due for a bed bath. You can do the honors." She laughed, as she turned to gather the soap and towels that I would need. "Come on, newbie, I'll introduce you."

Following Gloria down the hand-railed hallway, I noticed how the faded, worn floor was clean and polished. The open doors to the resident's rooms were adorned with wreaths made from silk flowers or grandkids paintings. The atmosphere was cheerful overall. Only the intermittent moaning heard from an occasional room broke the illusion. Most of these people were suffering from dementia, were stroke victims or were just extremely elderly. My job was to assist them with bathing, feeding and the toileting needs.

Alma was completely dependent on us. Even though she had dementia and was extremely elderly at one hundred and three years of age, she could still yell . . . and cuss like a sailor. Using a warm, wet, soapy washcloth, I gently washed her arms while she tried to scratch, and bite me, cussing with every exhale of breath. Using a clean, warm, wet cloth, I rinsed the soap from her wrinkled body and dried her with a warmed dry towel. When I picked up a comb to untangle her hair, she grabbed my arm. "Thank you," she said, looking me in the eyes and relaxing her grip. The old woman was momentarily replaced with a lucid person, who really appreciated my efforts. That was my true compensation for the day's work.

The rest of my shift was spent patiently spoon-feeding several residents lunch and doing rounds. A round consisted of changing soiled briefs and turning bed-bound residents.

At the end of the day, Gloria caught me by the arm as I was about to walk out of the door. "Hey, today is payday. You have a check for yesterday. Go get it before you leave," she said, turning to leave herself. "See you tomorrow!"

*Wow,* I thought, *I'm already getting paid.* All I had to do now was find a way to cash my paycheck. Even though it was for only one day, it seemed like winning the lottery to me. The sun seemed to shine brighter, the clouds casting smiles in place of shadows onto the sidewalk beneath my light-as-air footsteps. In no time at all, I found myself in front of the motel. I didn't know how much longer I would be allowed to stay with the "girls," but I was thankful for the cot and hot shower.

The hot steamy shower pelted the smell of soiled briefs and spilt, pureed food from my nostrils, giving my olfactory nerves a respite. Stepping out of the bath, I heard loud voices emanating from the other room. Wrapping a towel around myself, I surreptitiously peeked around the door. Doreen and Mary were glaring at each other. Mary was holding a small Starline cosmetic train case behind her back. It was obvious that they were arguing over it.

"You need to leave that here!" Doreen growled, holding her hand out toward the case.

"I don't trust her here! Mary responded vehemently. "I'm taking it with me. It'll be okay."

"And I don't trust you turning tricks using it as a pillow! That's just really stupid!" Doreen replied. Noticing me standing in the doorway with my towel dripping onto the blue tiled floor, Doreen said "She's a good kid. She knows not to touch anything."

Throwing the train case onto the bed, Mary snorted, "Fine. I guess you're in charge!" and stormed out of the front door, slamming it behind her.

Doreen turned back to face me. "Go on, get dressed, kid," she said, wiping her hand over her brow and smoothing her disheveled hair back into place. "I have a date, too. I don't like the idea of leaving you here alone, especially because Mary has a temper, and she told me that you have one more day or she's leaving." Frowning, she continued, "I can't afford this room by myself."

I glanced over at my bag sitting on the bathroom vanity. I almost said something about getting a day's pay, but hesitated. I really needed the money if I ever wanted to get out of there. So, I didn't say anything, I just turned and gathered up my clothes.

By the time I was dressed, Doreen was gone. The train case was nowhere in sight. Sighing and tired from the day's work, I sat down on one of the beds and turned on the TV. I was hungry but was too exhausted to do anything about supper. Leaning back onto the soft, plump pillows, I began to drift off to sleep, lulled by the murmured dialog from the TV.

I was jolted awake by a pounding on the door. Yawning, I thought, *Doreen must have left her key,* and I opened the door. Two men were standing there.

A tall, bulky man pushed his way in, causing me to stumble back. He averted my fall by grabbing my arm. "Where is the case, sweet cakes?" he growled through a tight smile that showed rotten teeth.

He was followed by a short, skinny man, who quickly closed the door after furtively glancing over his shoulder. "You look in the closet while I keep this little girl busy."

Rotten teeth man hissed. He let go of my arm and shoved me back onto the bed. With one hand around my throat and the other now gripping a gun he held against my temple he grinned as he questioned me. "Tell me where it's stashed, and I'll let you live."

Shaking my head, I whispered, "I don't know where it is!" I could hardly breathe, let alone speak, as his hold around my throat tightened. I was terrified that he would kill me. I felt my lungs struggle for the air that was not available. My world went black, and I felt a warm wetness between my thighs. My bladder had failed me. Losing consciousness, my fear was gone. Replaced with nothingness.

When I woke up gasping for breath, the two men were gone. The room was in shambles. Clothing was strewn all over the floor—torn from hangers—the drawers open and overturned on the floor. The bathroom vanity was swept clear of makeup; broken glass from perfume bottles littered the floor. I didn't know if they had found the case they were looking for and left or if it was still in the room somewhere. I didn't want to stay there to see what Mary and Doreen would do to me if it was gone. But if I left, they would think that I had taken it. Still shaking, I ran to the door and locked it. I changed out of my urine-soaked panties. I hung up the clothes and picked up the shards of glass from the bathroom floor. By the time Doreen came back I had calmed down some.

"What happened in here?" Doreen asked. "Are you ok?" She had noticed a darkening bruise where the man had shoved the gun barrel against my head.

Trying hard not to start sobbing, I told her what had happened. I described the two men.

"The skinny one sounds like Tina's pimp. I had a feeling that she was up to no good. She hasn't been back," Doreen snorted.

"They were looking for the train case. I don't know where you hid it, so I don't know if they found it."

Doreen gave me a glaring look and turned to the air conditioning vent underneath the table. She pulled the cover off and lifted the train case from its hiding place. "You are one lucky chick, it's still here." She opened the case revealing five stacks of bills bound with rubber bands. "And it looks like the money is all here." Looking relieved, she continued, "You know that when you leave in the morning, you can't come back."

That was fine with me. I hadn't planned on coming back.

CHAPTER 6
## A Real Job

MARY DIDN'T COME BACK TO THE ROOM THAT NIGHT. I really didn't want to run into her, so, as soon as the pink-stained fog of dawn was perceivable, I quietly left. Walking to work, I tried to come up with a plan on where to stay. By the time I arrived at the ivy-covered threshold to the nursing home, I was no closer to a solution. Greeting the housekeeper in the hall with a smile, I turned into the staff dressing room. Gloria was already there, dressed in her scrubs with a cup of coffee in her hand.

"Good morning," she greeted me. "Want a cup of coffee? I just made a fresh pot." With her smile replaced with concern, she gently touched the side of my head with her cool fingers. "Wow, what happened to you? You have one heck of a bruise!"

Sitting down with the cup of coffee Gloria had put in front of me, I felt that I could trust this woman, so I told her the whole story.

"Well, you can't go back there, you poor thing! Do you have anywhere that you can stay?" she asked me.

"No," I answered, "and I don't have a way to cash my check, and it's not enough to rent a room anyway." Looking down at my coffee, the steam wafting the aroma into my face, I sighed. "I don't know what I'm going to do."

"We can take care of your check. You can open a bank account at my bank, and withdraw the money you need." Now she was smiling at me. "Why don't you move in with me?" she asked. "We can split the rent. Maybe we can save money that way!" Looking pleased with herself, she said, "It's settled."

After a fulfilling day caring for our residents, Gloria ushered me out to her rusted, baby blue, Volkswagen bug. The door squeaked as she opened it for me. "Get in. Just throw your stuff into the backseat."

"What a cute car!" I exclaimed. "How old is it?"

"It's a 1960 model. I've had it for a couple of years. It's great on gas." Gloria beamed. Putting the car into gear and squealing away from the curb, she turned to me. "Are you okay? Is there anyone you need to call?"

"No, no one who would care," I answered. My future was in front of me. It was no use dwelling on past hurts. "Can we stop by the bank first? I'd like to open an account right away and get a little money for something to eat."

"Sure. It's only three thirty. The bank doesn't close until five," she replied. "We can go by the grocery store before we get home."

Home. That sounded strange to me; I had not had a home for a long while. Relieved, yet anxious, my hands were calm in my lap while my stomach was doing flips. I rested the back of my head on the back of the car seat and closed my eyes. The streets were all too familiar to me, having walked and thumbed my way along them. I knew instinctively where we were and which way we were going. Home.

Gloria's apartment was located beside a park. There were walking and biking paths that wound around a small lake. Eucalyptus trees, introduced to California from Australia during the Gold Rush in the 1850s, lined the paths and cast cool shadows. Their spicy fragrance filled the breezes. I found myself exploring the park on my days off, finding peace from my mind's torments. I almost didn't miss the drugs and alcohol.

The apartments were built in the 1950s. A lovely mosaic walkway, constructed from river rocks, led from the parking area to the front entrance. The building was a shoebox style, with balconies overlooking the park. Gloria's was a two-bedroom apartment carpeted in a green shag. Her furniture had a well-used appearance.

"You can sleep on the couch until you can buy a bed." Gloria told me. "The rent is $130.00 a month, so if split two ways, your half will be sixty-five dollars. Utilities are included in the rent."

I quickly calculated in my head. "That's only one week's pay! I'll be able to save up some money."

"Sure, but don't forget you'll need money for food and your part of the gas to get to work," Gloria reminded me. "You'll still be able to save if you are careful though."

* * *

The next few months went by quickly. I became proficient at my job and was even given the responsibility of training new employees. I was able to save up a few hundred dollars, even after buying a bed and bedside table from the nearby thrift store. I decorated my room with colorful, paisley-patterned curtains from the bargain bin. My weekends were spent walking in the park or on the beach. Life was good.

However, I missed my family at times. I dreamed about my daughter, wondering if she was okay. One day I decided to find out. I knew where my father and stepmother were living. I had copied the address from the telephone book into the journal I was keeping. They had moved from the house where I had lived with them. Borrowing Gloria's Bug, promising to fill up the gas tank, I started out one sunny, Saturday morning, with a map in hand.

My father had chosen a condo near the beach. It was an upscale, three-story, coral-painted, concrete and redwood shingled affair. The parking area was tucked underneath the building. I parked the bug on the street.

Walking toward the condo, my hands were clammy, and I could feel my heart palpitations. Taking several deep breaths to calm myself, I reached out a trembling hand to ring the doorbell.

My stepmother opened the door. Startled, she took a moment to realize who I was. As she started to close the door, my father came up behind her. "Who is it?" he asked her. He looked around her and saw me. "Hey, what are you doing here?" he stepped around her and opened the door wider. "Well, come on in."

I stepped into a room carpeted with gold shag. Looking furtively around the room, I caught my breath. Toys were strewn on the floor, blocks on the coffee table and several dolls on the floor. I managed to squeak out, "You have a nice place."

Gathering my courage, I continued, "Where is the baby?"

My stepmother glanced at the stairs. "She's taking a nap." Squaring her shoulders, she planted a smile on her face. "Do you want to see her before you leave?"

"Of course. That's really why I came," I bravely told her, standing straighter and looking her in the eye.

She missed seeing my resolve as she turned to go up the stairs. "Come on. You can see her room."

Following behind her, I felt as though I were in a dream. I couldn't distinguish if it was a good one or a nightmare.

The nursery was painted a cherry pink. A pure white canopy bed, draped with sheer, pink chiffon dominated the room. My two-year-old, tousled, blond daughter opened her eyes. Yawning, and clutching an obviously well-loved teddy bear, she smiled at us. "Mommy," she said . . . but not to me.

I felt as though my heart would break with joy, or grief, or the combination of both. "Hi, baby." I softly greeted her.

She held out her arms to my stepmother. Picking her up, my stepmother turned to me with a look of superiority in her eyes. "We need to get ready to go, sweetheart," she told the toddler. "We have an appointment soon. But thank you for stopping by," she told me.

Admonished, I went back down the stairs. My father was sitting on the couch in the living room. I picked up my purse and turned to him. "You have a real nice place here. And the baby's room is beautiful."

"Thanks, it's home," he said.

I grimaced at the word.

"Would you like a toddy for the body?" he asked. "I'm having one."

Remembering his term for a shot of whiskey, I nodded my head and followed him over to the bar set up in the corner of the living room. My stepmother appeared at the top of the stairs with my baby in her arms. "Are you ready to go, Daddy?" she asked my father.

"Almost," he replied as he poured both of us a shot. "Come on down. Find the car keys, will you? I think I left them in the kitchen."

My stepmother sat my daughter down on the couch and turned to find the car keys. I grabbed the opportunity to sit down beside her. "Hi, sweetheart." I smiled at her and was rewarded with a smile. I picked her up and sat her on my lap. My father had a Polaroid camera in his hand and took our picture. Taking the undeveloped picture out of the camera, he surreptitiously handed it to me along with a brown-liquid-filled shot glass. I put the undeveloped Polaroid picture into my purse, and gulped down the burning whiskey, just as my stepmother reentered the room.

Polaroid of author and daughter.

I stood up from the couch and gently sat my daughter down again. Handing the empty shot glass back to my father, I smiled at her. "I've got to go too. Maybe I can come visit again soon."

My stepmother opened the front door for me. "Please call us next time," she said frowning. Somehow, I knew there would be no "next time." I was not surprised when I found that they had once again moved, with no address listed.

\* \* \*

I threw myself into my job, volunteering for open shifts. I found a second job as a telephone solicitor, setting appointments for estimates on storm windows and siding. I was able to save enough money to buy a used car. It was a 1968 Firebird, dark blue with a black top; the interior was black leather. With a 5-speed manual transmission, it was fun to drive. Gloria and I took an occasional weekend during the winter to escape to Big Bear Mountain located in the San Bernardino Mountains. It was only a two-hour drive from our apartment. There was snow there, a welcome change from the never-ending summer season of the California coast. Even though my life was finally somewhat normal, I mourned the loss of my child . . . and my own childhood.

I had recently been in touch with a childhood friend living in Denver, Colorado. He invited me to come for a visit, and I eagerly accepted. I thought that by leaving California, I could leave my heartache behind as well. I was eager to experience four distinct seasons. As I looked around my room, I realized that all I wanted to take were my clothes and the picture my father had taken of me and my daughter. Everything else, my furniture and the few decorations I had collected, I gave to Gloria.

"I'll miss you." Gloria sniffed. She hugged me tight. "But I know that you think you have to go."

"I'll miss you, too. You are my best friend," I told her through my own tears. "You saved my life. God sent me an angel when He put you into my life."

We hugged once more before I opened my car door. "Don't forget to call me when you get there so I'll know that you made it safely," Gloria said. Waving at me as I pulled away from the curb, she watched me until I turned the corner.

CHAPTER 7

## *Evolving*

THE JOURNEY FROM THE APARTMENT TO MY FRIEND'S HOUSE in Denver was 1,010 miles. It would have taken me fourteen hours to drive straight through. When I saw the road sign indicating that I had crossed into Utah, I began looking for a place to park for a few hours. I pulled off the road and stuffed my pillow under my head. As daylight woke me, I squinted into the sunlight. Checking my map to be certain that I was headed in the right direction, I breathed a prayer of thanks and started my car. The drive was refreshing. The natural features of the landscape were breath taking. I found myself driving across a rugged terrain, punctuated by small mountain ranges. The sky was a brilliant blue. Clouds skimmed the distant mountain tops like white- and gray-tinged feathers. I was headed East and the sun shone into my eyes, causing tears to form and drip down my cheeks—mingled tears of grief and joy. It was too hard to discern the difference.

I didn't have to stop to eat. I had brought a small cooler filled with sandwiches that sweet Gloria had made, carrot sticks, apples and several jugs of water. I stopped only for gas—fifty cents a gallon—and to use the restroom.

\* \* \*

It took me two and half days to drive to Denver. The sudden magnificence of the Rocky Mountains startled me, rising from the desert, looming larger and larger, capped with snow. They were a severe contrast to the gentle, green mountains of North Carolina. Aroused from my half-stupor from the long drive, I eagerly pulled over to drink in the view and plot my route to my friend's house.

The traffic became denser, necessitating slowing down to maneuver. Searching the street signs, I finally found the one I needed. I hoped that my friend Frank was home. He was expecting me. As I pulled into the driveway, I had not even opened my car door when he appeared at the door. "Hey, stranger!" he called. "What took you so long? Really, you made good time."

I was so happy to see someone from when my life was innocence. I almost started to cry, but decided to smile instead. "Hey, yourself!" I greeted him. "The drive was long enough. You don't know how glad I am to be here!"

"Well, come in the house. You know my big brother, Rick. He's staying here for a while." Frank lifted my bag from the backseat. "You'll meet Tom. He's from here. He's a great guy."

Frank led the way through a messy living room to a back bedroom. "This is where you can sleep. There are three bedrooms, but only one bathroom. You know these old houses . . . cozy." He turned to give me a bear hug.

Frank, Rick and I sat down at the kitchen table and chatted about the old days and what we had been doing lately. I left out telling them about a lot of my experiences in California. I didn't want to think about the bad, only the good. And the good was here and now.

Supper that night was spaghetti with Frank's home-made meatballs. The sauce was Rick's contribution. I made the salad. We were like a family. More of a family then I had actually ever known.

The often-spoke-of Tom finally made an appearance the next day. He had a chess set in a carved wooden box tucked underneath his left arm, and his right arm supported a bag of groceries. "Thought I'd better come and meet your gal friend," he said while setting down the bag of groceries on the kitchen table. "Do you play chess?" he asked, turning to face me with a grin. "No? Well, never too late to learn."

He was tall, with long, chestnut hair pulled back into a ponytail, with a trimmed beard to match. Intense hazel eyes bore into mine, sending an unspoken dare. "Sure. I'm willing to learn," I answered him. I was attracted to him from the moment I saw him. The obvious fact that he was intelligent was evidenced by not only the patient way he explained the game of chess to me, but also by our conversations that lasted for hours. He had a wicked sense of humor. He came from a large, close-knit family that I came to know from frequent Sunday dinners. We became good friends.

The visit turned out to be a change of residence. Due to my experience working in California, I found a good paying job as a telephone solicitor. I was able to help pay the rent, the utilities and my share of the groceries.

* * *

Tom became a regular house guest. After six months of mutual flirting, we became a couple. Even though I had found love with Tom, my heart still carried a wound caused by the loss of my child. I discussed this through my tears with Tom.

He held me tenderly and asked, "What can I do, darling girl?"

Looking up at him, his face shimmering by my tears, I answered, "I want a baby. Could you do that for me?"

Stunned, he laughed, then became thoughtful. "If that would make you happy . . . but I'm not ready to be a dad."

"That's all right. I wouldn't need anything from you. I've been taking care of myself a long time. Just be my dear friend."

So, it was agreed, and ten months later I was five months pregnant, and living in Washington State. We had left Denver to get away from the crush of civilization. Tom had friends who were caretaking several hundred acres of land on top of a mountain in the Cascade Range.

Luke and Sue were true, down-to-earth people. They lived in a three-room log cabin with a loft, where Tom and I slept. We simmered lentils on top of a wood stove, and baked bread from the wheat Sue and I ground from wheat berries. Luke was an experienced mycophagist; he foraged for morel mushrooms. I enjoyed walking the woods with Luke, learning the difference between edible and unpalatable mushrooms and picking the tender, green fronds of fiddlehead ferns to go into the pan with the mushrooms. Along with herbal tea brewed with the clean, cold water from the pump well, we feasted on the gifts from the earth.

When the weather changed, and a warm spring arrived, Tom and I built a shelter outside from pine boughs. Dragging the large boughs was hard work. With perspiration dripping down his nose, Tom smiled at me. "The Finnish call this a Laavu," once more impressing me with his considerable knowledge.

I brought my armload of books on labor and childbirth, along with a blanket and pillows, to the shelter. It was pleasant underneath the fragrant pine boughs. I spent hours there, reading.

I was considering having my baby at home. The doctor I was seeing for prenatal checks, a Seventh Day Adventist, encouraged me. "Childbirth is a natural process," he told me. "Hospitals are for sick people, and you are a very healthy young woman."

Every trip to town for supplies was supplemented by the public library. I read everything available to me about home birth. Ina Mae Gaskin's book *Spiritual Midwifery,* Elizabeth Bing's *Six Practical Lessons for an Easier Childbirth* and *Thank You, Dr. Lamaze,* by Marjorie Karmel, were my guides. I felt prepared and more than willing to avoid the horror I had gone through giving birth at the hospital with my first child.

* * *

Tom began going to town alone several times a week. One night he didn't come home. I woke up that morning to find the bed empty beside me. Concerned and upset, I put my moccasins on and started walking down the road toward town. I had been skeptical of his excuse of having to call his mother from town because we didn't have a phone on the mountain. When I questioned him about why he had to call his family so frequently, he gave dubious reasons.

Sue saw me leave and ran to catch up with me. "Where are you going?" she panted, out of breath from jogging to catch up with me. "You can't walk to town," she exclaimed, knowing full well what was on my mind. "It's five miles down the mountain."

I was out of breath too, having run down the road a distance. I was cramping and doubled over as she caught up with me. I felt a warm wetness between my legs. Touching the wetness, I noted it was sticky, and when I brought my hand to my face, I saw bright red blood. I was only seven months pregnant!

"Oh, come back to the cabin, I'll brew you a cup of tea. You need to lie down and put your feet up." Sue scolded me. "You need to calm down. No man is worth it."

My anger gave way to fright at the sight of the blood. With Sue supporting me, we slowly walked back to the cabin. Tucked under a quilt with my feet up, a cold cloth on my head and one on my belly, sipping a cup of Shepherd's Purse and Nettle tea, I felt relieved that the bleeding slowed and finally stopped.

Sue admonished me to stay off my feet the rest of the day. "The baby is okay." Sue told me after putting her ear to my belly to listen to the heartbeat. "I want you drink two cups of tea every day now."

Thank the Lord, I didn't experience any more problems with my pregnancy.

Tom arrived back at the cabin two days later. My anger had cooled to disappointment. "Where were you?" I asked him, rubbing the swell of my belly protectively.

"I was visiting a friend," he answered. "You were the one that said you didn't need any help with the baby. So, I'm doing my thing."

Sighing, I realized I had not expected respect from any of the men in my life. After my parents had allowed me to be molested, I felt as though I was not worth being protected. My self-worth was absent. The only way I knew how to respect myself was to be strong, telling myself that I didn't need anyone.

\* \* \*

The next couple of months on the mountain passed quickly. Fall came and went in a moment. Winter was approaching, and Sue had reservations regarding the forthcoming birth. "I have friends that live in town. They would be happy to let us stay there until your baby is born. We'd be close to the hospital."

Sue's friends, Amy and David, were a Seventh Day Adventist couple. They didn't have any children or pets. Their house was sparsely furnished and clean, a change from the clutter and dirt floor of the mountain cabin.

Amy was excited to see us. She had been scrupulous in gathering supplies for a home birth. There were clean towels wrapped in foil, ready to be sterilized in a hot oven, scissors to cut the umbilical cord, new wrapped shoelaces to tie the cord, and lots of healthy snacks. "I have only to go to the store for lemons and honey," Amy said. "I have a recipe for 'laborade.' It will keep you hydrated." Comforted that this couple was willing, and actually wanting, to assist me gave me hope that maybe I was worth protecting. I knew that my baby and I would be safe. By giving birth at Amy and David's home, I would be avoiding the epidural and episiotomy I had endured with my first birth. I would be able to move around and not be tied to an IV or made to lie on my back in a narrow bed. Most of all, no one would take my newborn from my arms.

My labor began early one morning. Snow had begun to fall and drift against the holly bushes outside the bay window. It was a glorious day. The contractions were mild at first, like a clenching and unclenching of a fist. My back began to ache, and Amy had me lean over a pile of couch cushions while she massaged my back. In between contractions, I nibbled on scrambled eggs and cheese. The laborade was a sweet and salty lemonade. It quenched my thirst and seemed to give me energy. I felt cared for. This was a new feeling . . . love.

By twilight, just as the contractions started to feel intolerable, I felt the urgency to push. With Sue and Amy kneeling on either side of me, I squatted over a towel and felt a burning sensation. "It's your baby crowning; just blow, blow," Amy encouraged. "There's the head!" she exclaimed as she used the rubber suction-bulb syringe to suck out any amniotic fluid from my baby's nose and mouth. I felt a rush of fluid, along with my baby, gush from my body. Joy infused my soul as I reached for the wet, mucus-covered infant. After bringing him to my breast, safe in my arms, the four of us embraced warmly. "Thank you, oh, thank you!" I said to my friends and the Lord. With a cry of indignation, my newborn son nuzzled, head swinging back and forth, mouth open. Laughing, Sue told me, "He's rooting for a nipple. Let him suckle, it will help deliver your placenta and minimize hemorrhage."

I pushed the afterbirth out with minimal bleeding. Amy examined the placenta to make certain it was intact. "I'm sure you're tired," she told me. "After you eat some soup, I'll tuck you and your baby in to sleep. I'll be close if you need anything."

I woke several times just to watch my son sleep. He was so tiny and so perfect. "I'll call you Ezra," I whispered. I slept, knowing that angels were watching over us.

* * *

My son and I stayed with Amy and David for another month. They refused any money I tried to give them. "Use that money to start your new life," Amy insisted. "Just try to keep in touch with us. You're family now."

I wanted to go back to Colorado. I had fallen in love with the pristine air and magnificent views. I had friends there too. My car was covered with snow, so as David scraped the windows and shoveled the tires out, Amy helped me load my belongings into the back seat. She had packed a large basket of food and beverages for the road. With tearful goodbyes and warm hugs, we parted.

The drive back was another sixteen hours. My baby and I stayed overnight at a quaint roadside motel for one night. Stopping only to nurse and use the bathroom, I made good time. Finally, I found myself back in Denver at my friend Frank's house.

"Hi kid! Where's Tom?" he asked me. "And who is this little guy?"

"I left him in Washington, and this is my son, Ezra. Tom wanted to do his own thing. I'm doing mine. Do you mind if we stay here until I can find a place?"

"You know that you are always welcome," he said, too polite to mention Tom again.

We stayed at Frank's until I found a converted school bus that my son and I could live in. I thought that the bus was wonderful. The floors were hardwood, and there was a comfortable bed, table and chairs and a gas stove. I decorated the windows with calico curtains, and the bed with colorful throw pillows. During the winter I plugged a space heater into an extension cord that Frank had plugged into his outdoor electric outlet. We had a small Christmas tree decorated with the construction paper cutouts my son's chubby hands had fashioned.

Schoolbus kitty.

There was a communal daycare nearby. The parents traded time with each other caring for the children. This allowed me to go back to work. I was able to save most of my money because Frank let me park my bus on his property for free. We were happy, my son and I, we had each other. Living in the bus was fun, it was our own place. But it was becoming too cramped, and I started to think about my options.

## Chapter 8
# Disillusion

WHEN EZRA WAS NEARING HIS SECOND BIRTHDAY, I became more and more preoccupied with the certainty that he needed a father in his life. So did I . . . need a father in his life. I met a man at the local church we had begun to attend. He seemed to be an honest, God-fearing gentleman. He asked me to marry him after only a month.

Leaving my friends Frank and Rick for a man I barely knew was difficult. I really hadn't prayed on it. I should have. It is clear to me now, the men in my life have all been abusive. Was I attracted to this kind of man, or did I attract them by my victim persona?

I put my bus up for sale, trusting my friends to take care of it while I was gone.

The very day his wedding ring was on my finger, he became someone else. He dropped his pretense now that he had me legally. I once again found myself at the mercy of a violent man. He craved power and enjoyed my fearful reluctance by raping me often. There was no tenderness in his hands as he threw me down and tore at my clothes. He didn't care that my 2-year-old son was in the room.

My new husband was a construction worker. We never stayed long in one place; he followed the jobs. He moved us to Washington State during the aftermath of the eruption of Mount St. Helens. The dust covered everything. When I became sick from it, he refused to let me go to a doctor. I wheezed through my days and used a nasal decongestant at night to breathe.

I realized too late that I had made a dreadful mistake marrying him. Determined not to continue with this mistake, I waited until I knew that he would be gone all day. I quickly packed two small backpacks with both my son's clothes and a few of my own, making sure that the money I had saved while living in the bus was safely hidden in my bag. Ezra and I hurried down the driveway to the busy intersection where I once more stuck out my thumb.

God was looking out for us. The people that picked us up were angels. The first car stopped almost as soon as we reached the intersection. It was an elderly couple on their way home from visiting their children. "Where are you headed?" the woman asked me as she smiled.

"Denver," I replied hopefully. "Are you going that way?"

"Denver is over a thousand miles, child. We aren't going that far, but we can take you at least to the next town. In fact, you and your son should stay for supper, get a good night's sleep and get a fresh start in the morning."

Relieved, my heart beat settled down to a normal rhythm as we put the miles and my abusive relationship behind in the volcanic dust.

Supper was simple—a salad, hamburgers and chocolate ice cream for desert. My son and I settled down together on a generous couch and fell asleep.

Morning came too soon. Startled out of sleep by my son crying, it took several seconds to remember where we were. I had a desperate need to get farther away, feeling that by now, my husband was looking for us.

The kindly elderly couple offered us breakfast. I accepted a piece of toast and a carton of chocolate milk for my son, and a ride to the bus station. I bought a ticket to Denver and was lucky enough not to wait long. Twenty minutes later, my son and I were sitting in the back row of a Greyhound bus.

"Mommy, my tummy doesn't feel good," my son complained. Setting him on my lap, I watched him proceed to vomit chocolate. That was the only mishap. We made it to Denver safely. But by now, *my* stomach was cramping.

I called my friends from the bus station. Surprised by our sudden, unannounced arrival, Frank took my chocolate-covered, sticky child from my arms as I explained through tears what had happened.

"You know that you can stay with us as long as you want to," Rick said, as he put a brotherly arm around my shoulders.

Thank goodness, their home wasn't too far from the bus station. I was nauseated and had cramping in my lower back. I just longed for a real bed to rest in. Later that evening, after everyone had settled down to sleep, I was jerked awake by a sharp pain. Rushing to the bathroom, I had an overwhelming urge to defecate. Straining on the toilet, I felt a pop, a gush of fluid and a sudden relief from pain. Looking down, I saw a small balloon-like bag. I had miscarried. I had not known that I was pregnant. Saddened, but relieved, I was able to put that episode behind me. I had even finished this book, when I remembered this heartache, and decided to include it.

Soon, I filed for divorce. The court granted me an uncontested divorce after my abuser could not be located.

I have made so many mistakes in my life—out of ignorance, out of fear, out of need. But God forgives. If not for Him, I know that I would be worse off, or even dead now. The hard part is forgiving myself, and the people who mistreated me.

CHAPTER 9
# Riding on the Back

MY SON AND I HAD MOVED OUT OF THE CONVERTED school bus into an apartment in the very midst of the Garden of the Gods in Colorado Springs. The apartment building was constructed in the 60s. The countertops were a wonderful cherry-orange Formica, the carpets lime-green shag. We were on the second floor overlooking the valley of Manitou Springs, Pikes Peak snowcapped in the distance.

I had found work as a waitress at a local watering hole and pizza restaurant with a magnificent view of Pikes Peak. The sauce was made from scratch and the drinks weren't watered down. The bartender offered the wait staff leftover blended drinks from the bottom of the blender—cold frothy, tasty alcohol that fueled our smiles and patience with grievous patrons.

I paid Lori, a stay-at-home mother of six, recommended by a fellow waitress, to watch Ezra while I was at work. Lori was a lovely Christian lady with a husband who had a motorcycle-riding brother. One evening as I was leaving her house after kissing my son bye, a cute, blond, shirtless, tan man roared up on a Harley 1200. I couldn't help noticing flexed muscles as he swung gracefully from his bike. Throwing a smile my way through a thick, well-groomed, Viking red beard, he bounded up onto the steps and into the house where my son was still waving at the window.

On the drive to the restaurant, I smiled thinking about that smile. Oh, and of course, the tanned, shirtless chest. The rest of the evening was pleasantly spent with my customers, many of them on vacation. I offered suggestions on where to go and what to see locally. The tips were good that night. One table left me a $25 tip on a $20 check.

Suffused with a good mood, I picked up my son. Lori was excited. "My brother-in-law really wants to meet you!"

"You mean the blond guy on the motorcycle?" I asked. I hoped that I didn't appear too interested. Now I was really in a good mood! "Well, I guess you could give him my phone number."

* * *

His name was Chris. Originally from North Dakota, he was then living in Manitou Springs, a quaint little village outside of Colorado Springs. The warm springs were reputed to be healing. In the 60s, scores of hippies flocked to the springs seeking visions of peace and love. Their influence mingled with the native tribal presence to create seasonal festivals full of color and feathered dances. There in the town square, nestled between Pikes Peak and the rolling hills of high desert, people of all colors gathered to watch and participate in the dances and become of one creed.

* * *

Chris and I dated exclusively for several months, the taste of Carmex from his lips forever imprinted upon my memory. He took me on long rides through the mountains on the back of his motorcycle. I loved the wind that snatched up my hair and twisted it into dreadlocks. Leaning into the winding curves, spooning behind him, I thought that here was a perfect man. Ezra was now three years old and by all intents and purposes, fatherless. I had it in my mind that a male child would benefit from having a father in his life. So, I decided to see where this was going.

One glorious day, after riding to Cripple Creek and back, we went to his place nestled on a hilltop overlooking Manitou Springs. He unlocked the door and ushered me into a quaint rustic-style, three-room apartment. Taking off his jacket and draping it over the comfortable looking couch, he turned on his stereo. Electric Light Orchestra was playing "Strange Magic" as he smiled and took me into his arms. We kissed, slowly making our way onto the waterbed in the adjoining bedroom. Having been celibate for over three years and still in my twenties, it was not difficult to succumb to his embrace. In fact, I became passionate. I was feeling good, but he was repulsed by my enthusiasm. Turning away, he snarled, "This isn't working for me; you are too 'pushy.'" He told me that I wasn't "as good sexually as his ex-fiancée" and that is was due to my having been "used," meaning that I had already had a baby.

I figured later, *Maybe, he is turned on by the woman being victimized.* The more that I resisted, the better it was for him. Not only did he belittle me in bed, he criticized my parenting skills. My feelings were hurt, but I rationalized, maybe he is right. I was brought up in a family in which my father criticized my mother, so I thought it was a normal way to interact. Chris still hadn't hit me yet; that would come later.

I should have called it off then, but he asked me to marry him. My engagement ring had belonged to his ex-fiancée and was too loose on my finger. I protested having a previously worn ring and he had the diamond reset into a smaller band. We were married a year later. My wedding was outdoors, the minister a Seventh Day Adventist. My natural parents and step-parents didn't attend. They had never seemed to be interested in my life. I had wanted a bouquet of wild flowers, especially wild lilacs, but Chris and his brother had brought me a bouquet from the dumpster behind a florist shop. I was disappointed, but did not realize at the time how prophetic the act was. I was second-hand. After the ceremony, we got into an argument over—what, I don't remember—but he ripped my dress down the front in rage. You would think I would have had a clue then.

Now for a honeymoon: a trip in the truck camper to Northern Canada. It was May and still chilly that far north. Having lived in a school bus with my infant son, the cramped space of the camper wasn't too difficult to manage, but the marriage bed had to be shared with a 4-year-old. Chris didn't seem to mind, but I was extremely uncomfortable . . . and embarrassed.

In the wilderness, there were no conveniences. We bathed in a nearby stream and our toilet was a hole dug behind a bush. This didn't really bother me; it was the dead Canadian goose that my husband had shot that shocked me. Then he handed it to me, dripping blood, and ordered me to dress, pluck and cook it. It was a stringy, tough and wild tasting. Chris never seemed to notice my discomforts and was oblivious to my dismay (and gagging). He was joyfully playing Daniel Boone.

I had no privacy, cramped into an eight-by-ten-foot truck camper. Early one morning while the boys were asleep, I eased myself out of bed and stretched my leg over my son asleep between me and the door of the camper. The air was still chilled from the night's temperature of forty degrees. Mist was rising off the lake. Early bird loons were calling from the distant shore. Grateful for a respite, I took my clothes off, and, wrapping a towel around my goose-pimpled shoulders, I walked to the water's edge. I had no sooner dropped the towel and stepped into the lapping water when I saw in my peripheral vision, a stranger, camera in hand, stalking me. Shrieking silently to myself, I plunged into the thirty-degree water, attempting to avoid exposure. My early morning bath interrupted, I stood and retrieved my towel, dripping from where the end had dropped into the lake in my haste. Getting a better look, the stranger turned out to be my new husband, sans beard. He had shaved it off completely, revealing a chin unfamiliar to me. Nonplused, he proudly displayed to me his surreptitious polaroid, my fanny prominent in my naked splendor.

Displaying ignorance at my dismay of privacy-intruded-upon, he laughed, smacked my backside and attempted a kiss that met only air. The rest of the "honeymoon" was forgettable for me, although I'm certain that my son and new husband had a good time.

Not having a home of our own yet, we drove to Minnesota to Chris's grandparent's farm. There we parked the tuck camper and moved into their two-bedroom trailer. Grandpa raised pigs. Grandma baked bread, cookies, meat and potatoes. There were five meals a day served in her kitchen—breakfast of toasted homemade bread, fried meat and coffee at seven a.m. before going out to the barn; lunch of cookies and coffee at ten a.m. at break time; dinner of homemade bread, rhubarb jam, leftover meat and coffee at noon; then back outside to work. Another lunch of cookies and coffee at three p.m. and supper of meat and potatoes at six p.m.

The meat stayed on low in a crockpot on top of the counter all day. Grandma and I spent the day mixing bread dough, putting it into a large stone bowl to rise while we mixed together flour, sugar and butter for the cookies. Heavenly fragrances called the menfolk into the house for lunch. We all sat down together and talked and laughed together. Cleaning up the kitchen, I opened the silverware drawer to find mouse droppings underneath the spoons, in fact scattered all around the bottom of the drawer. Grimacing with concealed disgust, I wiped out the tiny hard pellets. Finally deciding to empty the entire contents and dumping the mouse debris into the trash. I then began to suspect that the faithful crockpot was probably weeks overdue for washing. The rest of the house suddenly revealed spiderwebs slung between door frames and dirt crusted into corners.

Up until then, I had not stepped inside Grandpa and Grandma's bedroom. The smell of old urine turned out to be coming from the mattress, sagging and stained. The most I could do was strip off the sheets and wash them. Chris shook his head in dismissal when I asked him to at least take it outside into the sun to air. "It would embarrass them," he said.

At lunch, I brought up the subject to Grandpa, not mentioning that I wanted to sun-dry the pee, only that it would freshen it up. He told a story of how years ago, he would put DDT on and under the mattress "to get rid of bed bugs." Apparently, this was a common practice. The consequences years later from this practice were devastating. Both Grandpa and Grandma developed large cancerous growths in their necks and succumbed to the disease a few years after we left the farm.

Time spent in Grandma's kitchen was educational. I learned to make bread from scratch, and my Ezra loved to help make cookies. He played in the flour, creating a dust storm that caused Grandma, normally stern, to smile and praise him for his creativity.

## CHAPTER 10

# Minnesota

MY SECOND SON WAS CONCEIVED ON THE FAMILY FARM. WE decided to leave the farm after his grandparents were hospitalized.

My husband found a farm closer to the North Dakota-Minnesota border. We were given free rent in exchange for caretaking. It was a cattle ranch with a lovely old, two-story house. The glass in the windows was wavy and reflected the sunlight into prisms of color. The walls were insulated with newspaper from the 1920s; a narrow stairwell led upstairs to an open floor plan. The chimney boasted bare brick protruding from the north wall. Large green bottle flies swarmed the tall windows. It took a week to clean. The kitchen had not been updated and still had the opening in the wall where the stove pipe once belonged. I had an electric stove; however, the sink was an original stone with the hand pump still attached.

Here I practiced and perfected the art of baking homemade bread. Punching, kneading, pulling and folding dough was cathartic for me, my arms covered with flour as my fists pushed into the satisfying warmth of the dough, flour dust itching my nose. White powder streaked along my cheek where I pushed a stray hair out of my eyes. And, oh, the fragrance of baking bread rolling up and through the air! The sweet memory makes my mouth water and my eyes tear.

Our meals were mostly from the small garden out back beside the clothesline. About once a week, the owner of the ranch brought by fresh cuts of beef wrapped in wax-coated paper. He was an elderly gentleman with overalls and mud-caked boots. Because he was aware of the mud, he stood in the mud room at the door, smiling and touching the rim of his hat, greeting me pleasantly and handing me a large bundle.

If only my husband was so thoughtful. I scrubbed and mopped the entryway floor every day. Living in the country, I soon learned the experience of dirt and mud was a given. Living on a farm where the cattle were evacuating their bowels and my husband trudging through the muck, I knew filthy boots were expected.

Expected also was taking shoes off in the mud room, hence its purpose and name. I had just finished with the mop, leaning over my baby-filled middle, wringing it out, when in stomped my husband, cow dung-covered boots. Dismayed that my just-cleaned floor now was mired in ugly stinking cow dung, I asked him to please take his boots off.

Huffing toward me, he replied, "I'm not going to take my boots off to go to the bathroom." Pushing me aside, he continued into the bathroom to pee.

I sighed. "You could've done that outside." Foot prints now marked his path on my newly mopped floor. I picked up my mop and cleaned the floor again.

\* \* \*

It was winter in Minnesota. Ten below zero. Snow a foot deep covered the ground. We had both an oil stove in the living room and a pot belly wood stove in the dining room. I liked to sit in my rocking chair beside the pot belly stove and read. My unborn babe would move, stretch and snuggle inside me while I warmed my feet propped up on the stool in front of me. We kept the wood stove stoked against the chill all night. My 4-year-old slept upstairs, tucked into his own, little bed among scattered toys left from the day.

My husband, the six-month belly and I slept in the bedroom behind the dining room wall. I was dreaming of warm sun and surf breaking on a Florida beach, while snuggling under heavy quilts, when I woke because of my baby kicking against my full bladder. Familiar with this nightly ritual, I got up to a room filled with choking smoke. Wide awake now, I ran to the stairway and flew up the stairs to where my son was sleeping. No smoke there. I touched the exposed chimney, fearing a chimney fire. It was cool to my touch. Seeing that, I stumbled back down the stairs to wake up my husband. He was difficult to wake, but finally opened his eyes and groggily stumbled out of bed. The source of the smoke that was rapidly flooding the house was coming from the wood box inside beside the door.

My husband had apparently tried to shove a log into the stove that evening, and not being able to fit it into the stove, just threw it back into the wood box. There it had smoldered for several hours before becoming life-threating. He yelled at me to open the door and quickly snatched up the offending log and pitched it outside onto the snow. It burst into flames when it caught the brisk wind. If not for my yet-to-be-born son, our family would have perished that night.

Spring finally came, mud replacing snow. Wild iris, along with the mint and asparagus, planted by settlers brought from Europe, began to green. We now had fresh spinach and onions from the garden. Our milk we bought from neighbors who had a dairy farm two miles away. It was raw milk with cream on the top, rich and nourishing. I skimmed the cream from the jar and churned it to make butter. To some of the milk I added yogurt, and setting it aside on the kitchen counter, made more yogurt. Breakfast was fresh-baked bread spread with homemade butter and yogurt sprinkled with berries picked that morning.

## Chapter 11
# Birth at Home

I PLANNED TO HAVE A HOME BIRTH. MY HUSBAND WAS pleased. There was no one nearby to serve as a medical attendant so I planned none, and Chris agreed, to save money. Armed with the knowledge gained from the first home delivery, I was prepared. My labor began with my water breaking, soaking my overalls. I was in the garden weeding around the tender, feathery carrot sprouts, and my amniotic fluid mingled with the black loam soil, staining my knees. Rising to my feet, I brushed the soil from my hands and called out to my husband. We had secured a promise from a neighboring couple who had a child a few years older than Ezra. They were to be there, out of the way, to keep Ezra occupied.

When they arrived, I was in full-blown labor, my contractions coming in a tide peaking in a crescendo of strength and ebbing away, so I could catch my breath. I made a nest of fluffy pillows and blankets on the living room floor. Close at hand were my birth bag and clean, dry, soft towels. The sunlight of mid-morning flowed through the ancient, wavy glass and painted rainbows on my naked belly. Time stood still for me, only resuming with each new wave.

My babe moved within me, nudging and pushing his head ever lower while I strained to grant him freedom. Dark stained fluid gushed from me as his head crowned. I told my husband to get the Dee Lee suction ready, but he was fixed in a trance, eyes wide, mouth agape. I caught my blue-tinged babe as he slid out and wrapped a towel quickly around him. Before he took his first breath, I had the suction in and the stained amniotic fluid out of his mouth and nose. When he finally gasped and opened his eyes, considering my soul, I knew I had seen him before, maybe in a dream. We named him John.

* * *

My summer days that year were filled with joy, washing cloth diapers in the old-fashioned washer and wringer and hanging them outside. The wind blew dry the diapers hanging on the line; they were stiff when I took them down to fold.

When John was two weeks old, my husband decided to move us closer to his parents. Chris's family still lived in his hometown of Hoover, North Dakota. Bereft of color in the winter months, unless white and gray are ideals of color, the bed of the ancient Lake Agassiz bloomed in the spring with wild, purple lilacs. The communities clustered with miles of flat prairie separating them. The roads were straight and intercepted with one another with precise measured miles. Home addresses were numbered with mileage and rural route numbers—population one person per five square miles.

Chris's mother, Gerta, was a German war bride, his father, Will, a WWII American soldier. Her accent was thick, and the air was thicker with Chris's father's smoke. Will always had a lit cigarette between the fingers of his right hand, while his left fumbled with the open pack for another.

Gerta was blond, rapidly turning to grey, her features strong boned, with skin like a fine scrimshawed clay pipe. Short of stature and of stocky build, she had strong, capable hands that were used to hard work. She regimented her garden rows into perfect groups of profuse green. Huge, sweet tomatoes grew on vines as thick as thumbs. Rhubarb plants—with their tangy, reddish concave stems topped with green, poisonous fanned leaves—towered above rows of storybook sweet peas. The gnarly, sweet carrots were large enough to sustain one throughout the harshest winter famine. And winters were often long and bitter cold in North Dakota.

Will, retired, passed the winter months at his desk, hidden in a cloud of smoke while writing letters to friends and family, commenting on the weather. Tall and once-handsome, his large hands, calloused and with nicotine-stained fingers, he was no stranger to hard work. Looking back, I realize that living in North Dakota was hard work.

We found an acre of land with a single-wide trailer in North Dakota. It belonged to a local, sugar beet farmer, who had used it to house Mexican workers during the summer. He needed the money; the banks were foreclosing and auctioning off a lot of the farms at that time. Farmers lost their homes and lands, some of which had been in the family for generations.

We bought the property for one thousand dollars, our entire savings . . . or so Chris told me. Moving day his parents Gerta and Will came to help. Ezra and I had been packing boxes for days and now labeled and taped; they were ready to be loaded onto the Chevy truck sans camper shell. Both my husband and his dad had disappeared, leaving me, my mother-in-law and 5-year-old Ezra to wrangle the boxes. The men reappeared and promptly sat down on the lawn chairs. I convinced my husband to help pick up boxes and move them to the truck, only after I reminded him that I had recently just given birth to his son.

## CHAPTER 12
# A New Start

SEEING OUR NEW HOME FROM A DISTANCE WAS exhilarating. Seeing the trailer from the outside did not prepare me for seeing the inside. The fact that the farmer had used this trailer to house his migrant workers was evident. Bare, stained mattresses were laid side by side throughout the living room and the bedrooms. First thing on the list was to get rid of them. Chris took it upon himself to tackle that job without prompting. The place took a week to clean. After scrubbing down the walls, doors, kitchen and bathroom, cleaning the carpet was the next chore. And what a chore! At the end of sweating through a one hundred-degree day, I had sucked up with a carpet steam cleaner, six buckets of black mud and long strands of blacker hair. Leaving the doors and windows open allowed the carpets to dry quickly. I had only to stand guard and swat the flies.

After the transformation, our new property was beautiful, situated on the elevated bank formed when Lake Agassiz dried up, creating rich black soil a foot deep. We could see for miles across acres of sugar beets, winter wheat and sunflowers. On the north and east side were tall cottonwood trees, planted as wind breaks, called shelter belts by the settlers a hundred years before. Underneath them grew stubby boxwood trees, home to all sorts of wildlife.

Ezra came running home one spring day with what he thought was a kitten. It turned out to be a baby skunk! Even young skunks have scent glands, it seems, and a tomato juice bath was in this boy's immediate future. Along with the cute critters, there were also nuisance ones—mice and rats as large as small cats. So, we acquired a cat. She excelled at catching and dispatching these unwelcome critters. She also was very fertile and gifted us with several litters of kittens. My son bonded with one solid black kitten, and he named her Smokey. Smokey followed him everywhere he went. We could see her tail waving above the tomato plants as Ezra went about his chore of weeding the garden. Alas, she also grew to become proficient in reproducing. Her first litter was the only one she would have. When her babies were born, she didn't know how to nurse them the first hours, and my husband, always an impatient man and sometimes a cruel one, took Smokey out to the shelter belt and shot her. My son and I called her and looked all afternoon. That evening, she came back, her head half shot off, pitifully crying. Stunned, I rushed my son inside. I confronted my husband and asked him, "Why?"

"She was stupid," he responded. "She couldn't take care of her kittens; we already have too many cats." Sick to my stomach, I rushed her to the vet sixteen miles away, but it was too late. She died in my arms, wrapped in a bloody blanket. I fed her kittens by expressing my own breast milk, and feeding them with a dropper every two hours. They thrived. We were able to find them good homes on a neighboring farm. There they would spend their natural lives earning their living by chasing and catching mice. Chris repeated this solution to an annoyance when he tired of the family dog. We never found him.

I ached for the safety of the smoky, blue mountains where I was born and raised. Such a lonely, scary feeling would come over me when I gazed over the flat terrain of the North Dakota prairie, so open and so vulnerable. I comforted myself in my children's laughter and the sweet black soil of my garden.

My garden was huge, with everything from asparagus to zucchini. In North Dakota, the growing season is short, but intense. All my plants grew fast and large. I could can dozens of jars of tomatoes and beans; the herb garden grew fragrant chamomile and large leafy comfrey. The raspberry hedge was four feet tall with ten rows of red juicy berries and very happy bees. I found peppermint and asparagus growing at the edge of the property, connecting me with the European settlers who once lived on this land. The wild plum tree put forth enough luscious, red plums to make jar upon jar of preserves for the winter with enough left over for snacking.

The summers were hot. Hot enough that the trailer became an oven. My children and I spent the day on a quilt, reading and playing together underneath the large cottonwood tree in the backyard. The neighboring couple had two children, both girls, close in age to my children. The oldest one, Bobbie, loved to climb trees with my oldest son, her light brown hair curling around her flushed cheeks. The younger one, Rebecca, had short, blond hair that clung damply to her head when she rolled up and down the small grassy slope in my yard. She was the child at my side in the kitchen most often. When it cooled in the evening, I set two in a red wagon while the other children ran alongside. I pulled them around the block for a ride as they laughed and mooed at the neighbor's cows. When we arrived at our own yard, they caught the lighting bugs that created a fairyland, winking blue and yellow light among the green grass. Floating up, the delightful flying insects put early stars twinkling among the tree branches.

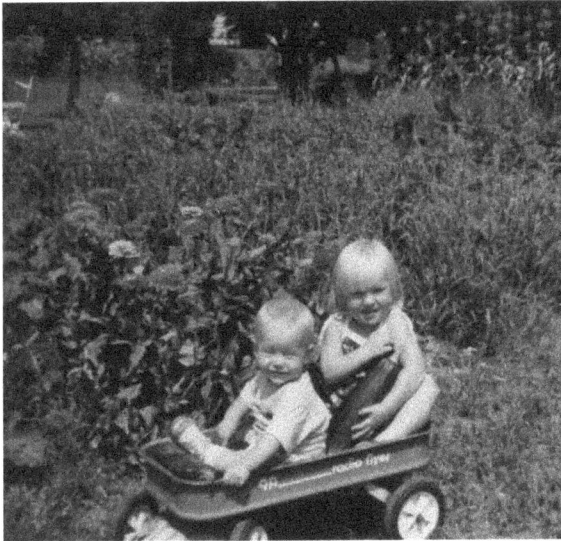

North Dakota kids.

The children became close companions, and their mother and I became close friends. I could confide in her. Later, my husband would blame her for the problems in our marriage, but she was part of my salvation.

112

* * *

Fall came early. We took the truck to a nearby shelter belt of trees and cut and loaded wood for the winter. There was an old potbelly wood stove situated between the open kitchen and the living room. It stayed lit most of the time and was a welcome warmth when the temperature outside dropped into the teens and below.

Two years after moving to North Dakota, I was once again with child. One February evening, it was twenty degrees below zero, and I was four months along. My husband came home late from a rod and gun club meeting. He was staggering and smelling of more than a few beers. I heard him come in, then I heard him cuss, then I heard a thud as he fell. Running into the kitchen, I could see his legs sprawled out in front of the wood stove. Coming around into the living room, I found him passed out, arm slung over a long, thick stick of cut wood, which was half in and half out of the roaring opening of the stove. The wood was a chunk of tie rod, called that because it was used to tie the metal rails of a train track together before being replaced by newer wood. We used these because of the heat they would put off when burned, being soaked with creosote used to preserve them. This one supporting my husband's weight was obviously cut too long to go into the stove. Another life-threating event from a wood stove and a too-long chunk of wood . . . and my husband.

Being heavy with child, I struggled to lift him off the log and let him just drop to the floor. It didn't faze him; he just continued to snore. That accomplished, I opened the kitchen door to help disperse the heat and smoke from the open stove door, the stoves pipe orange red and radiating heat in visible waves. I quickly filled jars of water in case they would be needed to quench any blaze. I then had to tend to the log, pushing further into the fire as it burned, taking at least an hour before it fit snugly enough to enable me to finally close the door to the wood stove. I sighed and went back to bed—disaster averted, my husband snoring, spread out on the living room floor in a drunken stupor.

\* \* \*

My newborn was a daughter! We named her Hanna. She was born on a hot and sunny July Sunday afternoon. My labor was short. I had wanted only my husband and two sons at home with me, but somehow the midwife I was apprenticing under got wind of my labor. She showed up unannounced, full of unwanted advice and unneeded offers of support. Without argument, my husband obeyed her orders and left the room. After only seven hours of active labor, my sweet dark-haired baby girl was born. She didn't cry, just looked up at me and rooted for my breast. We nursed as though we had done it forever. Wrapping my babe and me in my softest robe, I was aware of being ravenous. I told my husband, who had just walked back into the scene. His response, "What are you making for supper?" He was serious. Not one to ever joke.

I ignored him, sighed and snuggled with my daughter, embracing the heavenly, newborn fragrance of her sweet, soft, downy head.

My in-laws arrived, Gerta bringing her spicy and aromatic, homemade sloppy joes on a bun. I ate one while still nursing my newborn. Holding Hanna in my lap, I supported her tiny chin by my right hand, patting her back with my left. She let out a burp that belied her seven pounds. And it smelled like her grandmother's sloppy joe!

Thank the Lord for our church ladies. They hastily threw together a shower and supplied girlie clothes. Until then she wore only diapers and t-shirts. How wonderful to have a babe with a bonnet trimmed with ribbons! My toddler son had endured comments like, "What a lovely little girl." I had let his hair grow until he had blond curls down to his shoulders. Now that we had a daughter, his father insisted that I cut them off.

* * *

A few months later, I began to get sick. My nose stopped up completely, and I had difficulty breathing, wheezing with each breath. My afternoons found me so exhausted that I had to lie down. My doctor diagnosed asthma and severe allergies. We lived surrounded by wheat fields. When the farmers harvested the dry, golden brown stalks, they used a huge machine called a combine. It cut the wheat stalks, shaking loose pollen that filled the air with clouds of dust. This billowed over the fields and covered my fresh laundry with grit. I learned not to hang laundry on those days and to wear a wet bandana over my mouth and nose lest I choke to death. By Christmas I was very ill. My doctor diagnosed pneumonia secondary to the allergies.

My husband was less than sympathetic when I experienced any weakness. The scant amount of money that he allowed me to have each week was barely enough to keep the family in toilet tissue. The children wore clothes that I had made or that came from the thrift store. I was an avid coupon cutter and joined the co-op to save money on the food I could not grow.

One day I was on duty as a volunteer at the co-op sorting produce. I began to sneeze, and it was getting more difficult to breath. I realized that someone was in the back room grinding wheat into flour. Grabbing the children up, I rushed out of the door to the van. Before I became unable to breathe, I knew that I had to find an inhaler since I did not have mine with me. There was a pharmacy just around the corner from the co-op, and I rushed to the front door. Gasping for breath, I stumbled up to the counter. I was so weak from oxygen deprivation, I could not speak coherently. The pharmacist frowning at me noticed my blue lips and agitation. He interpreted my wheezing, understood and quickly handed me an inhaler. After a couple of puffs, my bronchioles relaxed their constriction. With color returning to my face and able to speak again, I thanked him profusely.

"No prescription, no payment needed, my dear. I couldn't let you die of respiratory failure in my store!" he responded. "I will just write it off as a defective one."

Thank you, Lord, for this angel of mercy!

## CHAPTER 13
# Breastmilk and Semen

IT WAS A COOL SEPTEMBER AFTERNOON. THE FARMERS HAD been busy baling up the dry hay, and my allergies were preventing me from going outside. My youngest child, Hannah, and I were resting from my morning chores. Snuggling next to me, she was nursing contentedly. I was lying on my side, with the phone cradled to my ear, talking with my mother. My husband came into the room, and seeing me on the bed, he decided to claim his rights as a husband. He climbed onto the bed behind me, lifted up my skirt and proceeded to fondle himself. Annoyed and occupied with both my mother on the phone and my nursing child, I told him "No, don't. Not now!"

He paid me no attention, and got busy.

"At least put on a condom," I whispered. "I might be fertile." He was already finished. This was not a new experience. He raped me all the time. Now there was nothing I could do but cry.

He got up and left the bedroom without a backward glance. Two weeks later, I knew that I was pregnant again. As my belly swelled with new life, my energy levels suffered. Waking up to prayer became my morning ritual. The herbs and organic vegetables growing in my gardens also sustained me. As a lay midwife, I continued to accept clients, couples wanting to conceive and needing my counsel, as well as women already carrying new life. Because my husband ignored me, it wasn't difficult to conduct prenatals at my home or to travel to the expectant parents' homes. He was almost always gone—supposedly hunting or at work. When he was at home, I was afraid that I or the children would say or do something to anger him. My children went with me to these prenatal visits and the home births. I found my joy once more, while Chris was more interested in visiting the women who lived alone in the neighborhood. "Doing odd jobs and fixing things." My bulging form was apparently not sexually appealing. That was fine with me but also saddened me to suspect that he was unfaithful. We kept up appearances, attending church every Sunday, a normal loving fruitful family.

## CHAPTER 14

# In-Laws and Outlaws

Life in the country was sweet, and my life became filled with the season's gifts. I prayed to God for some love to appear, and He answered me. I was apprenticing with the lay midwife who had attended my daughter's birth. My time became filled with expectant mothers and their babies. I became a primary midwife when one young woman asked me to attend alone her first baby's birth. She became a lifelong friend. I decided I needed additional training and became an emergency medical technician and then a nationally registered paramedic. The community appreciated my skill.

My in-laws never mentioned my accomplishments. I believe they disapproved of my catching babies at home. My husband never complimented me either. He often made disparaging remarks or just ignored me. If not for the little money earned from the midwifery, my children would not have had any Christmas presents, and their clothes would have been homemade or second hand.

We often went to his parents' house after church for dinner and to play endless games of Yahtzee or cards. I always felt out of place. But to defend somewhat my husband's behavior, that family was never demonstrative in affection. Norwegian culture? I felt stifled and lonely.

We decided to replace the sagging single-wide trailer with a new modular home. Doing most of the prep work ourselves, we rented a back hoe to dig the basement. It was cool and damp in that hole. While smoothing out the walls, I found ancient shells and what appeared to be clay beads. Excited, I showed my discoveries to my husband. He was not interested. Drain tile in place, we poured the concrete walls, covering up history.

The house was nice and brand new. Although I noticed that cheaper door knobs and tile were used, it was still a three-bedroom, two-bath home. Excited, my children and I went in to inspect the house.

\* \* \*

We spent several sweet years in that house. Now we had room for a decent Christmas tree as the living room ceiling was vaulted. The problem now was convincing my husband to buy a tree. He didn't approve of spending money on "unnecessary" things. Christmas trees and presents were unnecessary, in his opinion. I was the one who bought presents from Santa each year from the little pay I received for catching a baby. One year, bereft of any disposable income, I lugged a huge, round beautiful tumbleweed into the house. The children and I decorated it for Christmas. We thought it was our most wonderful tree ever!

I carried a beeper for the local ambulance company I had volunteered with. My escape from tension at home was when it went off and I had to leave to assist them. I often arrived in my little silver bug before anyone else, stabilized the patient and was the one credited with saving a life. Late one cold night, my beeper went off. There was an accident not even a mile from the house. I grabbed my responder bag and quickly crunched through the snow to my car. Undulating ribbons of blue and green lit up the northern sky. The northern lights were breathtaking, but I had no time to admire them. Someone's life was at stake. The incident occurred on the neighboring farm, along the field road. Apparently, the farmer's son and his friends had been drinking and had decided to race their cars. One car had become mired headfirst in the ditch, throwing the farmer's son out over a fence into the field. When I arrived, he was unresponsive, with agonal breathing . . . slow, very shallow irregular respirations. I stabilized his head, making sure that his airway was open, and put an oxygen mask on him. Covering him with a blanket to minimize exposure to the cold, I sat with him in the snow to wait on the ambulance. He survived, and after weeks in the hospital, he graduated from high school with honors. His father was so grateful. He surprised me one evening. With tears in his eyes, he handed me a small velvet pouch. "Thank you for saving my boy's life!" he told me. When I opened the pouch, I saw several small diamonds.

"You don't have to give me these," I said. He insisted that I take them. That gift helped me later.

Those experiences and my midwifery were so fulfilling. Doing this work, I received the respect I was so longing for. If my marriage had not been loveless, I could not have asked for anything more.

* * *

It was winter. It had stormed that day and the snow was waist deep. My neighbor was expecting her third child the following month and planning on a hospital birth. When the phone rang late that evening, I was already grabbing my bag before my son answered it. It was my neighbor's husband, frantic that the birth was eminent. Thankfully, their farm was only a short walking distance because our car was buried. It was slow, difficult going, trudging through the snow. Gusts of cold wind pelted me with fine, stinging snow making my eyes water and my nose run.

Before I even opened their kitchen door, her husband was screaming for me to hurry. Following his voice, I ran from the warm kitchen to the back bedroom. The fragrance of birth permeated the room—the smell of fresh blood and perspiration. The mother was on her back on the bed with her knees bent and between her legs was the amniotic sack, the baby inside. I quickly noted the color of the membrane and snatched a feeding tube, the first thing at hand. With my umbilical scissors, I cut open the sack. As the meconium-stained fluid spurted out, one hand cradled the baby, the other wiping off the nose and mouth. I suctioned out thick, green meconium several times from the baby's trachea and spit it out of my mouth until nothing further was recovered. I wrapped the baby boy in a warm, dry towel, and after making certain that he was breathing and pinking up, I attended to the mother and the afterbirth. The ambulance arrived by dawn and transported mother and baby to the hospital.

The family thanked me. My husband and his family never mentioned it. When the subject came up, they made disparaging remarks like, "How stupid it is to encourage women to have home births." I encouraged women only to make their own decisions after educating themselves.

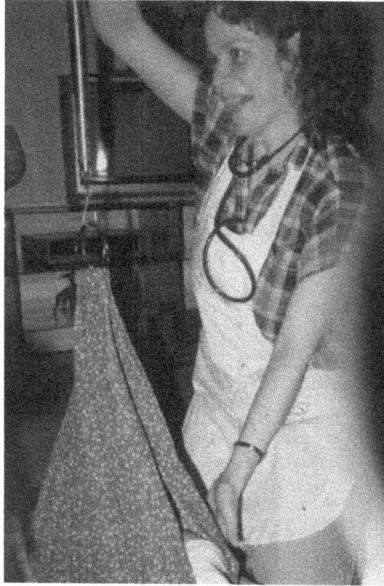

Author weighing baby
delivered at home.

We always tried to have a yearly family picture taken. I remember one year I put on lipstick. My husband became enraged. "Wipe it off!" he demanded. "You look like a slut." He made me button my blouse to the top button. I felt as though I was living in an Amish household.

125

The Sunday that I went into labor, I woke up with a nagging backache. "I really would rather stay home; I don't feel well," I told him, rubbing the small of my back and beginning to feel slightly nauseated.

My husband looked up from the task of putting on his boots and snarled at me. "You're going. Now get the kids ready." Then without looking back, he walked out of the door. He was already outside starting the car as my children and I were still searching underneath the couch for missing shoes.

Walking eased my aching back. *Okay*, I thought, *I'll make it through this.* The day was warm and sunny, and so that was the reason for the perspiration on my forehead, I tried to convince myself. After the sermon, handshakes at the door and cheerful farewells, we climbed back into the car to head home, or so was I was hoping.

Without a word of explanation, my husband turned onto the expressway toward town, a 45-mile drive. He then turned his head toward the backseat—where I usually sat with the younger kids—and he said, "We're meeting my parents for lunch."

"Great," I murmured, as the ache in my lower back became insistent. Not able to get comfortable, I fidgeted, turning from side to side to relieve the increasing pressure. "I think I'm in labor," I told him.

"Well, you're the midwife, aren't you?" he growled.

"Well, it feels different, no real contractions, just this backache and some nausea," I replied.

"You probably just ate a bug with your herbs." He laughed. "You're fine. You just need some real food." Somehow, he always managed to subdue me.

The restaurant his parents had chosen was a buffet. That made the children happy. They could eat greasy, fried chicken and sweet, gooey sundaes. Usually I limited the amount of junk on their plates, but today was an anomaly. I definitely was not feeling well. I scrutinized the salad bar selections and decided on a small helping of greens and crackers, hoping that the crackers would ease my stomach. As soon as I sat down at the table with my plate, I had a sudden urge to urinate. Excusing myself, I clumsily got to my feet.

My three-year-old daughter announced, "I have to go potty, Momma." She trotted behind me to the ladies' room.

Tearing off four-inch lengths of toilet paper and bending over to place them on the rim so that my daughter would have a clean seat, I felt a sharp pain shoot through my back. Sweat beaded my brow, and my hands trembled as I helped her up.

"You okay, Mommy?" she asked, sweet concern in her baby voice.

"I'm okay, honey," I lied.

When she had finished "tinkling" and with bottom dried and panties up, it was my turn. Telling her to wait for me, I repeated the ritual of lining the toilet seat with paper. Sighing, I sat down. With a great relief of pressure, I heard fluid gush. The lower back discomfort I had been experiencing all morning paused for few seconds, and then seized me around my abdomen. All right, now I know I'm in labor. My water had broken in the ladies' room at Golden Corral.

Returning to the table, I quietly informed my husband, "My water just broke."

Nodding his head, he returned to his interrupted conversation describing his newest gun to his father.

Irritated, I poked his back to regain his attention.

"You can wait until we're finished eating, can't you? You have hours of labor ahead of you." I didn't know at the time how prophetic his words were. I managed to eat a little bit of my salad and crackers. Eventually, the meal concluded with no mention of my leaking water to my in-laws.

My husband did not mention it at all on the long drive home.

With contractions occurring sporadically, I managed to dress the children in their play clothes. After sending the older two outside to play under their father's inconsistent supervision, I lay down with my youngest for a nap. Even though I felt exhausted, I was jerked awake by sharp, intermittent pain. It felt as though my pelvis was breaking in two.

Supper was a simple affair. Unable to stand long enough to cook, I served sandwiches. The children were satisfied, but my husband grumbled. "You must be getting slack. You know that I like a hot meal for my supper."

I reminded him that I was in labor.

"Really? Well, let me know when you are ready to get it over with."

* * *

The children put to bed, stories read, I slipped into the bathtub full of warm, soothing water. Soaking the day's stress away, I noted the pain of the strange contractions were easier to deal with. This was my fifth labor. I thought it would be familiar, but instead it was frightening. I felt that something was wrong. I gingerly climbed out of the bath and sat on the toilet. More amniotic fluid trickled out. Standing up and peering into the bowl, I saw bright red blood. This was not like the other labors. Worried, I tried to wake my now snoring husband.

He raised his hand in a gesture like he was swatting away a fly. "Lie down, you're fine, go to sleep," he said.

The contractions became more painful, insistent with pressure on my bladder making me trod to the bathroom with each one. The pain was now centered in my pelvis, my pubic bone feeling like it would rupture. When I wiped, bright red blood stained the tissue. I tried repeatedly to wake my husband. I wanted to go to see my doctor. Something wasn't right. The pain and bleeding continued all through the night.

When dawn finally arrived, the morning sun in his eyes finally woke him. Again, I impressed upon him the urgency of the situation. Yawning, pulling on his clothes, he was obviously recalcitrant, not wanting to getting up to help me. I called my neighbor to stay with the children, picked up my birth bag and made my way slowly to the car. It was a hatchback, the back just large enough for me to lie down. Sighing with relief, I relaxed.

Twenty minutes later, halfway to town, I felt my baby suddenly turn inside me, the sharp pain changing into pressure. "Stop the car! The baby is coming!" I yelled.

Pulling over to the side of the road, my husband opened the hatch of the car.

"Grab the towels, and my birth bag," I panted. My greatest fear was a hemorrhage from the long labor—38 hours. My shepherd's purse tincture, an herbal treatment for bleeding, was in my bag, and I had it out before my baby daughter slid out into the world. Her little arm preceded her head, her wrist bruised from being shoved against my pelvis during endless contractions. She had been presenting posterior, head down but facing my abdomen, her back to mine instead of the normal position. The blood was from my cervix being squeezed between her arm and my pubic bone.

She opened her eyes and looked around, a bit blue but healthy. I did not hemorrhage, thank goodness. Cuddling her to my breast, I began to nurse her.

Grinning, my husband got back into the car, turned around and headed back home. "No need to pay a doctor now." He smirked. I didn't care. I had my newborn Lilly in my arms.

When she was only a few weeks' old, my brother called me to tell me that our father had suffered a heart attack and was hospitalized. "You don't have to come," he told me. "You would just be in the way."

Despite the neglect from my father, I still wanted to go to him.

My husband agreed with my brother. So, I stayed home and held my children tighter. With the death of my father, I did not feel the need to keep the secret . . . and no longer feared my stepmother's threat to cut my throat with a rusty knife. My firstborn, now 18 years old, would know the truth. I called her. Leigh was living in California, going to college for her master's degree while working full-time as a store manager.

I didn't come right out and tell her that I was her biological mother. I told her my story and how I ended up in California, that her mother was my stepmom and that I was pregnant at the time. She was silent for a moment. Then she gasped as the truth dawned on her. "You all lied to me my whole life!" She was angry with everyone for years. It was such a relief for me to finally face the facts. I didn't want to hurt her, but I explained why I could tell her now.

* * *

With four children, ranging in ages nine to newborn, my days and nights were full. Along with the garden, housework and cutting wood to prepare for the winter's ten-degree temperatures, I was still expected to submit to my husband. There was no pleasure in our intimacy for me. I endured his rough and, thankfully, quickly ending embraces. Whenever I voiced my reluctance for intercourse, he became physically abusive, shoving me up against the wall and ripping my clothes. I avoided him as much as possible and was thankful when he was gone for hours at work or at his gun club meetings . . . or so he told me.

One evening he came home with a disheveled man, stinking of days-old sweat, alcohol and urine. The man was a hitchhiker who Chris had picked up on his way home.

"I'm fulfilling my Christian duty," he proudly announced. "Show him to the bathroom and to give him clean towels for a shower," he ordered.

As I prepared supper for us all, I was startled by the man stepping up close behind me.

"Yum, that sure smells good, ma'am." He sniffed the air at the back of my neck. "And so do you."

When I turned with my heavy soup spoon in my hand, I noticed that he had washed his face, his scraggly beard still wet. An aroma of body odor still clung to him. So much for a shower.

He stepped back when he heard my husband walk into the kitchen. "I sure do thank you kindly for the hospitality." He grinned at my husband . . . and winked at me when my husband looked away.

* * *

After supper, I asked my husband, "Are you driving him to town before it gets dark?"

"He's staying the night," Chris replied. "Get some blankets and a pillow for him; he can sleep on the couch."

"The man makes me extremely uncomfortable. I'm frightened of him," I said.

Chris shrugged me off like an annoying fly. Without responding, he turned and walked away.

That night I could barely sleep, waking up frequently at the slightest noise. I was feared that the hitchhiker would rape me and kill us in our sleep.

In the morning I got up early to prepare a bag lunch for him. It was only after the two men had pulled out of the driveway and were headed toward the highway that I was finally able to relax.

* * *

A month later Chris brought home another stranger—another homeless man he had found near his place of work.

134

"I told him he could have a good, home-cooked meal and a warm place to sleep tonight," my husband boasted.

Having not received a call ahead of time, I had to add another jar of home-canned tomatoes to stretch the pot of chili that I had made for supper. At least this man did not stink of gin and despair. He appeared to be grateful and thanked me for the bowl of hot chili I placed in front of him. He bowed his head and silently gave thanks. Relieved, but still cautious, I prepared the couch for him to sleep. The next morning, he was still asleep when my husband was leaving for work.

"Aren't you taking him with you?" I asked.

"No, he can stay here today. I told him that he could chop the wood for me." He walked out the door without another word.

So, my children and I were left alone with a strange man, miles from any neighbor within shouting distance. I fixed breakfast for us. We had pancakes with butter churned from the fresh, sweet milk that our dairy neighbors provided on a weekly basis, ripe strawberries from my garden and bacon from another neighbor whose hogs always took blue ribbons at the fair. The homeless man was truly grateful.

"Thank you, ma'am. I can't remember when I had a more delicious breakfast." He excused himself and asked me to please show him where the wood pile was. He chopped wood all morning. After a glass of lemonade and a sandwich, he told us goodbye. With a wave and, "Thanks again!" echoing after him, he was off down the road with his thumb out.

I was not aware of the tension that had made my shoulder muscles stiff and my fingers clinched until he was out of sight. I hugged my children and made up my mind to have a stern discussion with their father when he got home from work that evening.

Nervous but determined, I confronted Chris after supper. "I don't feel that it is safe to bring strange men home, especially to leave the children and me alone with them.

Frowning at me, he said sarcastically, "It looks like we won't have to chop any wood for a while."

I lost a little more of my respect for him at that moment. We never mentioned it again. At least he never brought any unknown guests home again.

* * *

We were like strangers living in the same house. I was apprehensive when he was home, trying not to turn my back to him. One time while I was washing dishes, he came up behind me. Laughing, ugly, he reached around me and grabbed and squeezed my breast. Hard. Pain shot through me as I hunched away from his groping. Mortified, tears forming, I tore away from his grip and ran to the bedroom. As I attempted to lock the door, he pushed his way in.

"What's the big deal?" he snarled. Disgusted as I was by his insensitivity, I still capitulated and said, "It's okay; my breasts are just so tender. I'm nursing, you know."

Huffing, he turned and walked out of the room.

When I returned to my sink full of lukewarm, still sudsy water, I was still wiping tears away from my eyes.

When my youngest turned 3, my husband came home with beer on his breath. I was at the kitchen sink, peeling potatoes for supper. He came up behind me and, grabbing the knife from my hand, held it to my throat. My 3-year-old was standing beside me. She said, "Daddy, don't hurt Mommy." It was then I decided the time had come to make a change.

My neighbor suggested that I see a counselor. I found a rape-and-abuse crisis counselor at the local shelter for women in town. She shed a lot of light on not just this relationship, but my past relationships as well. They all began as normal relationships, some too good to be true. But then my partners began to blame me for things beyond my control and point out my faults. They evolved into a draining of my self-worth, alienating any support systems. They left me feeling trapped and miserable.

She educated me in the ways of abuse. I needed someone to point out the warning signs. There can be a lack of communication, leading me to feel defensive all the time. Humiliation is a form of abuse; subtle jabs and insults are meant to make me submissive and to control. I should feel confident and encouraged by my partner. I should feel safe and protected, not threatened. The abuser shouldn't dismiss my life passions; he should encourage them. He might compare me to prior partners and always try to sabotage any friendships that I might have, even female friends and family. Acts of cruelty to animals is an established link between violence to pets and family members.

She thought my life had been threatened and that I should take steps to protect myself and my children.

* * *

My nighttime ritual occurred after my boys were in bed. I lay down with the girls who shared a bed.

I nursed my youngest and fell asleep with them. This was my excuse for my absence from the marriage bed. I could not tolerate even the idea of lying next to him. I was always apprehensive that he would force himself on me.

Chris began to work out of town more and more often. I had been waiting for an opportunity to pack up the kids and leave. He finally took a job out of town where he would be gone for at least two weeks. This was the opportunity I had been waiting for. Friends loaned me their truck, and with their help, the kids and I loaded some necessary household items, toys, clothes and boxes of pictures onto the truck. I knew that Chris would be furious when he got back home, but I couldn't face another day under the same roof with him.

My rape-and-abuse social worker, whom I had been seeing for the past month, had located an apartment in town close to my children's school. The rent and utilities were based on income. I had friends who knew the owner of the local café. A position as a waitress and cook was waiting for me. It was easy to relocate my family; but it was difficult to deal with Chris when he returned.

The first night after Chris had arrived home, he found out where we had gone. He came to the apartment and threatened me, pushing the door open and shoving me up against the wall. I tried to calm him down by saying that I just needed some space, that I had to think. He didn't leave until the next-door neighbor came over and threatened to call the police.

He changed tactics and attempted to appear caring. I would find the snow scraped from my windshield. Instead of feeling any positive emotion, I felt threatened. There would be no reconciling. This went on until spring. When school let out for the summer, I had saved up enough money to move far away from him. I told him my plan to go back East to my mother's home. Instead of being upset with me, he calmly told me, "Okay, you can take the girls, but you cannot take my boys." He even wrote a letter to that effect, giving me permission to take our daughters out of the state.

I knew he had always paid more attention to the boys and was genuinely concerned with their well-being, while ignoring the girls and concern for me.

I was anxious to get away from him. Every night while I was living so close to him, I went to bed frightened that he would suddenly appear, forcing me to have sex with him or slapping me around. I told myself, *I will send for my sons when I get settled back East.* Little did I know then that he would never allow that to happen.

I bought a station wagon for four hundred dollars and packed it with only what was necessary. I hugged and kissed my sons goodbye and told them that I would see them soon.

The drive was a lengthy one. We stopped only to rest and get something to eat. My mom was expecting us and was happy to see the girls. My stepfather was very happy to see me.

Several days after we had arrived at my parents' house, the girls were outside playing in the yard, chasing butterflies. My mom had gone to the store. I was in the house alone with my stepfather. He approached me hesitantly, and, given our history together concerning the sexual abuse, I expected the worst. Instead, he asked me to sit down. Sitting across from me, he sighed and said, "I hope that you can forgive me. I know that I ruined your life. I'm so sorry."

Surprised, I took his hand in mine. "You know, I couldn't forgive you. I tried. Then I prayed that God would give me the forgiveness toward you because I couldn't." With tears forming in both our eyes, I continued, "And He did. I do forgive you." My stepfather passed away five years later. It was extremely difficult for me to put a lifetime of self-deprecation behind me. I learned that finding acceptance and forgiveness for others' trespasses opened a universe of possibilities. By focusing on today while striving for tomorrow, I finally recognized my inner strength. Yesterday's lessons were learned the hard way. In my case, perhaps the best way. I was able to forgive myself for the many things I did to squelch the pain for the abuse and abandonment.

I was free from being intimidated. I no longer cringed at the slightest noise or walked around with my shoulders hunched over. Even though my ex-husband never consented to giving me custody of my sons, we worked out an arrangement. The children would spend alternate summers together, with either him or myself. It wasn't the greatest, but at least we made it work. He married the woman I had suspected he had been seeing while we were still together.

Working part-time to support my daughters, I went back to school first for my GED, then for my CNA, then for my nursing license—thanks to a Pell grant. I never remarried.

My children survived to adulthood, and my firstborn moved closer to me. We are finally family. They have all become successful in their chosen profession. They all found spouses, and now I have nine, beautiful grandchildren. My daughters and I took care of my mother as she was dying with cancer. It brought us closer. I was able to forgive my mother, too, for not believing me. She never wanted to discuss it, so carried my forgiveness in my heart. As she was lying on her deathbed, I told her.

Over the years, I have been in close contact with my sons and have traveled many times to North Dakota to see them and their families.

Life is still difficult at times, but the homelessness, abuse, loneliness and terror are behind me. The days begin, no matter sun or rain, with a thankful heart.

# Afterword

I realized after my experiences and after delving into research by professionals, that I had a "double whammy." I was abused by my stepfather and abandoned twice by my biological father and then, my mother. It has taken years to process, to understand how that trauma affected me. Now I am finally feeling I can be in a position to help others.

I've learned that in order to be whole, forgiveness is key. After learning the full extent of the wrong done to me and the major impact it has on the brain of a developing child, I was able to forgive others who were responsible for that trauma inflicted on me. Then, as my own advocate, seeing what had governed my behavior, I could finally forgive myself for whatever I once felt personally responsible for. It's not a quick fix; there is no magic spell to cast away years of pain. I am still working on forgiveness. Every new day is an opportunity.

* * *

Here are some things I came to understand:
**Childhood Sexual Abuse:**

Incest is the most common form of childhood sexual abuse. "Sexual abuse occurs whenever one person dominates and exploits another by means of sexual activity or suggestion."[1] Ratican defines childhood sexual abuse as "any sexual act, overt or covert, between a child and an adult . . . where the child's participation is obtained through seduction or coercion. Irrespective of how childhood sexual abuse is defined, it generally has significant negative and pervasive psychological impact on its victims."[2] Women who had experienced familial abuse reported higher levels of depression and anxiety. Maltz states that childhood sexual abuse infringes on the basic rights of human beings. Children should have sexual experiences at the appropriate developmental time and within their control and choice.

1. Maltz, Wendy. "Treating the sexual intimacy concerns of sexual abuse survivors." *Sexual and Relationship Therapy.* Abingdon, UK and New York, N.Y.: Routledge, 2002, vol. 17(4), p. 321-327.
2. Ratican, Kathleen L. "Sexual Abuse Survivors: Identifying symptoms and special treatment considerations." *Journal of Counseling & Development.* 1992, vol.71(1), p. 33-38.

When sexual abuse occurs in childhood, it can hinder normal social growth and be the cause of varying psychosocial problems. Higher levels of depression, guilt, shame, dissociative patterns, repression, denial, sexual problems and relationship problems occur. Survivors may have difficulty establishing interpersonal relationships, such as establishing boundaries, exhibiting passive behaviors, and getting involved in abusive relationships.

Maltz lists sexual symptoms that often result from abuse: "avoiding, fearing, or lacking interest in sex, approaching sex as an obligation, experiencing negative feelings, difficulty in establishing or maintaining an intimate relationship."

Helpful goals for the survivor may be to increase sense of control and increase ability to accurately attribute responsibility. It is vital to process, uncover and express anger because anger can be used to help the survivor feel empowered, appropriately attribute responsibility, establish boundaries, and promote self-efficacy and power.[3]

## Father-daughter abandonment:

3. Van Velsor, P., Cox, D. "Anger as a vehicle in the treatment of women who are sexual abuse survivors: Reattributing responsibility and accessing personal power." *Professional Psychology: Research and Practice.* 2001, vol. 32(6), p. 618-625.

According to Caitland Marvasco, as quoted in the website of wehavekids.com/family-relationships/, When a father rejects his fatherly duties entirely, his absence leaves an indelible mark on a daughter's psyche as she grows into adulthood. "Fathers provide their daughters with a masculine example. They teach their children about respect and boundaries and help put daughters at ease with other men throughout their lives. So if she didn't grow up with a proper example, she will have less insight, and she will be more likely to go for a man who will replicate the abandonment of her father."[4]

Consequences that are often related to fatherlessness for daughters are low self-esteem, depression, promiscuity and unhealthy male relationships. The absence of a father can cause his daughter to abuse drugs to ease the pain. According to the U.S. Department of Health and Human Services, fatherless children are at a dramatically greater risk of drug and alcohol abuse.[5]

---

4. Maravasco, Caitland; https://Wehavekids.com/family-relationships/"When-Daddy-Dont-Love-Their-Daughters-What-Happens-to-Women-Whose-Fathers-Werent-There-for-Them".

5 U.S. Department of Health and Human Services. National Center for Health Statistics. Survey on Child Health. Washington, DC, 1993.

\* \* \*

Later, in nursing school, I learned that extended exposure to traumatic situations, such as profound neglect or sexual molestation, could manifest itself in denial, depression, chronic pain and a myriad of other impacts on an individual's daily coping mechanisms and responses to daily life.

\* \* \*

If you or anyone you know is experiencing abuse, there are numerous local agencies that can give you information, support and safe harbor.

My hope is that by reading this story, someone's life will be spared the anguish I endured. I couldn't prevent the exploitation I suffered. But a reader may avoid the pitfalls that followed. I was really abusing myself with the drugs, suppressing my pain and anger. But meeting the prostitutes shook me up. Instead of defaulting to a life walking the streets, I could see I needed to take control of my life and not allow natural feelings—from needing a father and requiring retribution for my exploitation—permeate my being. I was ready to make my own decisions and not have my life decided by others.

– Yours in peace,
M.A. Sandry

Author's five children together.

# Acknowledgments

Thank you to: Rick, my love, who keeps our home fires lit. The sisters of my heart: Meg, my first primary home birth mom and a forever friend. Mardell, my apprentice and my soul sister. Amy, who stood with me weathering the storm. And Micki, my publisher, whose persevering instruction and enduring work made this book possible.

www.ingramcontent.com/pod-product-compliance
Lightning Source LLC
Chambersburg PA
CBHW042339040426
42448CB00019B/3334